Selected PEARLS From the Word

Selected PEARLS From the Word

Barbara White Hege

BLADENSBURG,
MD

Selected Pearls from the Word

**Published by
Dove Christian Publishers
P.O. Box 611
Bladensburg, MD 20710-0611
www.dovechristianpublishers.com**

Copyright © 2019 by Barbara White Hege

Cover Design by Mark Yearnings

All rights reserved. No part of this publication may be used or reproduced without permission of the publisher, except for brief quotes for scholarly use, reviews or articles.

Scriptures quotations, unless marked otherwise, are from the King James Version of the Bible (public domain).

ISBN: 9781732112582

Printed in the United States of America

Dedicated to these gifts from God:
Lisa, Rachel, Anna, and Riley.
Romans 12:1-2

Contents

Dedication v
Chapter 1 1
Assurance
Chapter 2 10
His Peace
Chapter 3 14
Sacrifice
The Holy Spirit
Chapter 5 20
Sin has Consequences
Chapter 6 23
Prayer
Chapter 7 32
Cleaving
Chapter 8 35
It is All About God
Chapter 9 40
Soothing Balm
Chapter 10 43
Giving
Chapter 11 47
Victory
Chapter 12 50
Agape Love
Chapter 13 56
Forgiveness
Chapter 14 59
Joy
Chapter 15 62
Do Not Fear
Chapter 16 64
God is Sovereign
Chapter 16 67
Stand Strong and Pray

Chapter 17 73
Unlovely People
Chapter 18 76
How Should We Live?
Chapter 19 81
Hope
Chapter 20 84
Thanksgiving and Praise
Chapter 21 89
Seasons of Life
Chapter 22 91
Home

Chapter 1
Assurance

Occasionally, I meet Christians who have no assurance of their salvation. That may seem like a strange statement. How can you be a Christian and not be assured that you are God's child and will be with Him eternally when you die? I believe it is because we mix works with grace. I did that for several years. If we look honestly at ourselves, we realize we fall short of being all God wants us to be. Because of this, we are fearful. How can we be sure? How can we not be afraid that, somehow, we will miss the boat?

We are going to examine some scriptures and see what God has to say. This should settle the issue, as God's Word is truth. It is where we should always go to seek the truth and for any questions we may have concerning God and His provision for our salvation, who is Jesus Christ. The Bible tells us that faith comes by hearing the Word. Therefore, if we want more faith and less fear, where should we go? We should go to His Word, reading and praying, trusting God to teach us and increase our faith.

We need to keep our eyes on Jesus and not on ourselves. Hebrews 12:2 reads, "Looking unto Jesus, the author and finisher of our faith, who for the joy that was set before Him, endured the cross, despising the shame, and is set down on the right hand of the throne of God." This tells us very plainly that Jesus is the author and finisher of our faith. He began it, and He finished it. He planned for our salvation before we were born (Titus 1:2). Jesus carried out that plan on the cross of Calvary and then rose from the grave on the third day and later ascended to heaven. As He died on the cross, He said, "It is finished." In other words, He did not leave anything undone. He did everything that was or is necessary for our salvation. He did not do half the job. He did it all, leaving nothing for us to do but to believe and receive this free gift.

When I was growing up, we had a saying: 'once and for all.' That meant something was over—finished. Nothing else was to be done. Hebrews 10:10 uses that similar illustration: "By the which will we are sanctified through the offering of the body of Jesus Christ once for all." It is done. Verse 12: "But this man, after He had offered one sacrifice for sins forever, sat down at the right hand of God." Jesus' work was finished, and He sat down on the right hand of God. Verse 14: "For by one offering He hath perfected forever them that are sanctified." How long does this say we are perfected? Forever! And how are we sanctified? "... through the offering of the body of Jesus Christ". Did He say we are sanctified by how we live or what we do? No! We are perfected and sanctified by His offering. It is all of Him. Can we give Him praise?

Ephesians 2:8-9 says, "For by grace are you saved through faith, and that not of yourselves. It is the gift of God, not of works, lest any man should boast." Could it be any plainer? We are not saved by works or how we live. It is only by the grace of God through faith in Him. It is a free gift. It is given because "God so loved the world that He gave His only begotten Son, that whosoever believeth on Him should not perish, but have everlasting life." John 3:18 says, "He that believeth on Him is not condemned: but he that believeth not is condemned already because he hath not believed in the name of the only begotten Son of God." This does not mean how we live is not important. How we live is very important, but it is not how we are saved. It should be the result of our salvation. There will be more on this later.

Titus 3:4-5 reads, "But after the kindness and love of God our Savior, toward men appeared, not by works of righteousness which we have done, but according to his mercy He saved us, by the washing of regeneration, and renewing of the Holy Spirit, which He shed on us abundantly, through Jesus Christ, our Savior, that being justified by his grace, we should be made heirs according to the hope of eternal life." Notice it says, "not by works of righteousness which we have done." How then? "According to his mercy, He saved us." It is not by something we have done, but what He has done for us. Regeneration is to be renewed, restored. We are renewed by the Holy Spirit He has given us. We are justified by His grace. This is all of Him and nothing of us.

John 10:28-29 says, "And I give unto them eternal life, and they shall never perish; neither shall any man pluck them out of my hand. My Father, which gave them me, is greater than all; and no man is able to pluck them out of my Father's hand." We are so very safe and secure with God and Jesus. No one can ever take us out of His hands. There is no safer place we could be than with them and in their hands.

If we could live righteously enough to go to heaven, Christ need not have come. If we could be good enough on our own, Christ died in vain. But we cannot. We are born sinners, and there is nothing we can do about that. But a loving God did something about it for us. He provided a way for us to escape hell and judgment. That way, and the only way, is Jesus Christ. He bore our sin, paid our penalty, and freely gave us eternal life. We, who believe, are the redeemed, bought and paid for by the precious Son of God; by His blood; His death, burial, and resurrection. Romans 4:16 reads, "Therefore, it is of faith, that it might be by grace, to the end that the promise might be sure…" For the promise to be sure, it must be of God. If it depends on us, it would not be sure because we are unholy on our own and often fail.

The Bible tells us that Abraham staggered not at the promises of God through unbelief, but that he was strong in faith, giving glory to God, and it was imputed to Him for righteousness. *Imputed* means to ascribe goodness to a person as coming from another. This same righteousness that was imputed to Abraham is imputed to us through Jesus Christ. The Bible teaches that we are righteous only in and through Him, and not in ourselves.

> **Romans 3:21-22 explains, "But now the righteousness of God apart from the law is manifested, being witnessed by the law and the prophets, even the righteousness of God which is by faith of Jesus Christ unto all and upon all them that believe."**

We are given the righteousness of God through Jesus Christ. It is imputed to us just as it was imputed to Abraham.

> **Second Corinthians 5:21 says, "For He has made Him, who knew no sin, to be sin for us, that we might be made the righteousness of God in Him."**

How are we made the righteousness of God? We are made the righteousness of God through the sacrifice of Jesus Christ bearing our sins on the cross of Calvary.

> **Romans 3:20 "Therefore by the deeds of the law, there shall no flesh be justified in His sight."**

He tells us plainly in this verse that we are not and never will be justified by how we live or by keeping the law. Verse 24 tells us exactly how we are or can be justified:

> **"Being justified freely by His grace through the redemption that is in Christ Jesus."**

We are justified by His grace through Christ Jesus. It is all of Him and nothing of us. Allow me to say it again: it is God's plan, God's doing, and nothing of us. He did it all, and it is finished. All the praise, honor, and glory belong to Him and Him alone.

He continues to tell us in the fifth chapter of Romans that sin came upon us by one man, Adam, and then judgment.

> *"...Even so by the righteousness of one, the free gift came upon all men unto justification of life. For as by one man's disobedience many were made sinners, so by the obedience of one, many shall be made righteous"* (Romans 5:18b-19).

How does it say we are made righteous? By the obedience of Jesus Christ. He shed His blood on the cross that we might be made righteous. He lived a perfect life, one that we cannot live. He did it for you, for me, and for all who repent and believe in Him.

> *"If his children forsake my law, and walk not in mine ordinances; if they break my statutes and keep not my commandments; then I will visit their transgressions with the rod, and their iniquity with stripes. Nevertheless, my loving-kindness I will not utterly take from him; nor allow my faithfulness to fail"* (Psalms 89:30-33).

There are consequences to sin; to our disobedience of God. Chastisement will come when we stray, just as we punish our children when they disobey. We do this to teach them the best way to live and because we love them. But they are still our children.

In the book of Exodus, when Moses and the Israelites were in Egypt, God told Moses to instruct the Israelites to take a lamb and kill it. They were to strike the lintels and side posts of their home with the blood of the lamb.

> Exodus 12:12-13 says, *"For I will pass through the land of Egypt this night, and will smite all the firstborn in the land of Egypt, both man and beast. I will execute judgment. I am the Lord. And the blood shall be to you for a token upon the houses where ye are; and when I see the blood, I will pass over you."*

This is called the Passover, mentioned in Exodus 27, and points to Jesus Christ. 1 Corinthians 5:7b also refers to the Passover, saying, "For even Christ, our Passover, is sacrificed for us." When judgment came to the Egyptians, how did the Israelites escape that judgment? They escaped only if the blood had been applied. It is the same with you and me today. When we accept Jesus and put our faith in Him, the precious blood of the Lamb, Jesus Christ, is applied and covers our sins. Colossians 1:14 says, "In whom we have redemption through His blood, even the forgiveness of sin."

> *"These things have I written unto you that believe on the name of the son of God, that you may know that you have eternal life"* (1 John 5:13).

We know because we believe God and believe His Word. A popular children's song is "Jesus Loves Me." According to this song, how did we know Jesus loved us? *For the Bible tells me so.* We believe what His Word tells us. That is part of our faith—trusting Him and His Word.

> *Ephesians 1:13: "In whom ye also trusted, after that ye heard the word of truth; the gospel of your salvation; in whom also after that ye believed, ye were sealed with that Holy Spirit of promise..."*

> *Ephesians 4:30: "And grieve not the Holy Spirit of God, whereby ye are sealed until the day of redemption."*

We are sealed by the Holy Spirit, who lives within us. We are safe and secure, now and forever more. We are sealed by the Holy Spirit, and no one can ever break what God Himself has sealed.

> *Psalms 32:1-2: "Blessed is the man whose transgression is forgiven, whose sin is covered. Blessed is the man to whom the Lord imputes not iniquity."*

Again, in Romans 4:3-5:

> *"For what saith the scripture? Abraham believed God and it was counted to him for righteousness. Now to him that worketh is the reward not reckoned of grace, but of debt. But to him that worketh not, but believes on Him that justifieth the ungodly, his faith is counted for righteousness."*

> **Verses 7-8** *"Saying blessed are they whose iniquities are forgiven, and whose sins are covered. Blessed is the man to whom the Lord will not impute sin."*

Hear what the Word says. If salvation comes by works, it is not grace. But it comes only by grace, freely given through our Lord and Savior, Jesus Christ. Our sins are covered by the precious blood of the Lamb.

> **Colossians 2:13:** *"And you, being dead in your sins and the uncircumcision of your flesh, hath He made alive together with him, having forgiven you all trespasses."*

How many trespasses has He forgiven? It says ALL trespasses. That includes past, present, and future. All means there *ain't* no more. Excuse the bad English, but it gets the point across. Does this give us a license to sin? No!

> **Romans 6:11-12, 15** *"Likewise, reckon ye also yourselves to be dead to sin, but alive unto God, through Jesus Christ, our Lord. Let not sin, therefore, reign in your mortal body, that ye should obey it in its lusts... What, then, shall we sin because we are not under the law? God forbid."*

We are to walk in obedience to God, but when we sin, we confess it in repentance (1 John 1:9) and receive forgiveness.

> **Acts 13:38-39** *"Be it known unto you, therefore, men and brethren, that through this man (Je-*

sus) *is preached unto you the forgiveness of sins; and by him all that believe are justified from all things, from which ye could not be justified by the law of Moses."*

How are we justified? Through Jesus. And from how many things are we justified? All things. By the shedding of His blood, He covers it all. Always and forever, salvation; forgiveness of our sins is all of Him and nothing of us. Blessed be His holy name.

Romans 11:29: *"For the gifts and calling of God are irrevocable (or without repentance)."*

God does not take away what He has freely given. What would you think of a friend that gives you a gift and then takes it back? Not a lot, I suspect. *Irrevocable* means it cannot be taken back; it cannot be undone. God is much greater, holier, and more loving than any friend we could ever have. So why would we ever think He would take away what He has freely given?

2 Corinthians 9:15: *"Thanks be to God for His unspeakable gift"* (Some translations use "His indescribable gift").

John 10:28-29 (Jesus speaking): *"And I give unto them eternal life; and they shall never perish, neither shall any man pluck them out of my hand. My Father, which gave them me, is greater than all; and no man is able to pluck them out of my Father's hand."*

We see again that eternal life is given to us as we believe in Him. No one can ever take us out of our Father's care.

Romans 8:38-39 *"For I am persuaded that neither death, nor life, nor angels, nor principalities, nor powers, nor things present, nor things to come, nor height, nor depth, nor any other creation,* *shall be able to separate us from the love of God, which is in Christ Jesus, our Lord."*

Oh, hear and believe what He is saying. NOTHING will ever separate us from the love of God, which we have received through Jesus Christ. What a Savior!

On that high note, I feel I must go a step further and make something clear. When we believe in Him and receive Him into our hearts and lives, we become His children. That is position. Our walk is a different matter. I do not mean to imply that we are secure and should walk in disobedience to Him and His Word. The Bible says in Galatians 5:25:

"If we live in the Spirit, let us also walk in the Spirit."

2 Corinthians 5:15: *"... that they who live should not henceforth live unto themselves, but unto Him who died for them, and rose again."*

We are now to live our lives for Jesus Christ. In walking in obedience to Him, we can have joyous fellowship with Him. When we disobey, the fellowship is broken until we repent and confess. We can live victorious lives through the power of the Holy Spirit if we submit ourselves, our lives and hearts to Him, His Word, and His Spirit. He saved us to make us free and no longer bound by sin. He says in John 10:10 that He came that we might have life and have it more abundantly. May we live free and abundantly!

Chapter 2
His Peace

How can we know the peace of God? How can we have peace that passes all understanding? Here are some scriptures that will help us do just that.

> **Romans 15:13:** *"Now the God of hope fill you with all joy and peace in believing, that you may abound in hope through the power of the Holy Spirit."*

As we walk in obedience to God and submit to the Holy Spirit, He works in us and grants us this peace. We cannot and will not know this peace if we walk in disobedience to Him and His Word.

> **Philippians 4:6-7:** *"Be anxious for nothing, but in everything by prayer and supplication, let your requests be made known unto God. And the peace of God, which passes all understanding, will keep your heart and minds through Christ Jesus."*

When we walk in sweet fellowship with Him, we experience His peace, which is so great, it is beyond our understanding.

Do we realize that worry is sin? The above verse tells us not to worry; "Be anxious for nothing." How do we keep from worrying about a loved one that is ill; one that is facing difficulties of some kind; one who has not accepted Jesus Christ into their heart and life; or one who has, but is walking in disobedience to Him? How do we keep from worrying about situations in our own lives? He tells us in this verse. As we pray for them and whatever situation they (or we) are facing, we then leave the results to God. We can thank Him that we can trust our loved ones with Him. We can trust Him with any situation that comes. He loves them even more than we do. He loves us more than we can imagine. As we pray and yield our worries to God, we can know His peace. God will work it out in His time and His way. It is all part of trusting Him. He is ever trustworthy. He is able to do more than we could ever ask or think.

Do you know that in the midst of whatever calamity may come, God is undisturbed? Do you wonder how that can be? That can be because of who He is. He is the master of any storm, calamity, or whatever befalls us. We need to remember that. Sometimes we just need to take the time to sit before Him with whatever our problem is; just sit there before Him, for however long it takes, and receive His peace, His calmness. He knows; we are His, and we are not alone. He is for us and with us.

> *Philippians 4:8: "Finally, brethren, whatever things are true, whatever things are honest, whatever things are pure, whatever things are lovely, whatever things are of good report; if there be any virtue, and if there be any praise, think on these things."*

We are to think on these things rather than the things we cannot change while praying and trusting God with the results. We should think of things for which we can be thankful. We should praise God for His love, His mercy, His grace, and so many other things. Just look for God's goodness all around us and in our hearts and lives.

> *1 Peter 5:7: "Casting all your care on Him, for He cares for you."*

What an invitation and a blessing! Almighty God invites us to cast all our cares upon Him. We don't have to carry these burdens. We can leave them with Him. Could they ever be in better hands? Absolutely not! We are to look beyond our circumstances. We are to keep our eyes on Him and trust Him with our loved ones. We should trust Him with any and all cares of this life. Why? Again, He tells us in this verse, "because He cares for us." We can trust Him in all these things. We can trust the one Who gave His only Son for us. We can trust the one who says in Jeremiah 31:3b, "Yea, I have loved thee with an everlasting love…" It is a glorious statement of fact. His love for us is eternal. This is another gem from His word that causes our heart to swell with thanksgiving and praise.

> **Isaiah 26:3: "Thou will keep him in perfect peace whose mind is stayed on thee."**

This reminds me of Peter when he walked on the water. As long as his eyes were on Jesus, he was fine. But when he looked at the situation instead of Jesus, he began to sink. We are to focus our minds, thoughts, and eyes on God. Then we can rest in Him and know His perfect peace. Think on Him. Think on His Word. There is comfort, strength, help, peace, guidance, and so much more to be found there. He knows all about our troubles and cares. He cares. He will work it out or lead us in doing so. When assailed with doubts or worry, remember Peter. Don't look at the situation. Look at our God and Father who is far greater than any situation or worry we could ever experience.

> **Isaiah 48:18 "Oh that you had hearkened to my commandments. Then had your peace been like a river, and your righteousness like the waves of the sea."**

Hear God's heart in this scripture. He desires for us to obey Him. He desires for us to experience this peace. We experience this peace as we walk with Him in obedience to Him and His Word.

> **Job 22:21 "Acquaint yourself with Him, and be at peace."**

This is telling us to get to know God. We do this much the same way we get to know another person. We get to know them by spending time with them, by talking to them, and by doing things with them. So, it is with God. We need to spend time with Him by praying (talking) to Him and reading His Word. We should yield ourselves to Him and His Holy Spirit, who comes to live in us when we become His children. We walk with Him in obedience to Him and His Word. The more we do this, the better we know Him, and the more we know Him, the more we know beyond a shadow of a doubt that we can trust Him.

Ephesians 2:14: "He (Jesus) is our peace."

We have that inner peace of knowing Him; that He is ours and we are His. We are assured that someday, we will live with Him throughout eternity. We have fulfillment that can only come from knowing Him.

Before coming to Him, I always had a longing for something more in my life, for something I could not quite figure out. But after coming to know Him and yielding my heart and life to Him, I realized that He was that something for which I had always longed. In Him, I found that fulfillment and peace I had never known before.

Chapter 3
SACRIFICE

> *"I beseech you therefore, brethren, by the mercies of God, that you present your bodies a living sacrifice, holy, acceptable unto God, which is your reasonable service. And be not conformed to this world, but be ye transformed by the renewing of your mind, that ye may prove what is that good and acceptable, and perfect will of God"* (Romans 12:1-2).

Have you ever thought of your body as being a sacrifice to God? Yet that is what He is saying. We give/yield ourselves, our lives, our bodies to God to serve Him and others according to His will and not our own. We no longer live to please self; we live to please God, to know Him, and to worship Him.

Abraham placed his son, Isaac, on the altar before God. I believe that is what God is telling us to do. We place ourselves on the altar before God, willing to serve and obey Him. Our lives are no more our own, but we, heart, body, and soul, are given to our Lord and God.

When we receive salvation through Jesus Christ, the Holy Spirit comes to live within us. We are not conformed to the world anymore but transformed. How are we to be transformed? We are transformed by the Holy Spirit who works in us as we read the Word, pray, and yield our bodies, our hearts, minds, and souls in obedience to God and His Word. He is the great teacher, teaching us and transforming us when we are in submission to Him. I do not mean to undermine faithful preachers of the Word. I love them and am so thankful for them. But the greatest teacher is the Holy Spirit. However, His teaching does not happen by osmosis. For Him to teach us and to begin transforming us, we have to be in the Word and in submission to Him and that Word.

Romans 12:12 tells us we are to rejoice in hope, be patient in tribulation, and to continue diligently in prayer. God is with us; He is here whenever and wherever we need Him or whenever we just want to talk. Talk to Him about anything. Pray about everything. He loves us. He wants to hear from us. We should remember to give Him thanks and praise often for all He has given us in Christ Jesus, for all He still does in our daily lives. He alone is worthy of all honor, glory, and praise.

> **Romans 13:14: "But put on the Lord Jesus Christ and make no provision for the flesh, to fulfill its lust."**

How do we make no provision for the flesh to fulfill its lust? Be mindful of our need to obey at all times and in all situations. Flee the temptation to sin. Do not go anywhere where we will be tempted to sin. Do not read or watch anything that brings sinful thoughts or desires. Be wary of friends who might lead you into sin.

Be sensitive always to the Holy Spirit, who lives within us. He will convict when temptation comes, but we must hear and obey. When He convicts us of sin, we must be willing to turn from it. We look to God and the Holy Spirit to help us do this.

> **1 John 1:9 "If we confess our sins, He is faithful and just to forgive us our sins, and to cleanse us from all unrighteousness."**

When tempted by the devil, Jesus used scripture to answer Him. This is what we should do. Rebuke temptation by quoting scripture that pertains to that particular temptation.

> "Neither yield ye your members as instruments of unrighteousness unto sin, but yield yourselves unto God, as those that are alive from the dead, and your members as instruments of righteousness unto God" (Romans 6:13).

Now He is more specific in telling us to yield not only ourselves but also the members of our bodies. We are to serve Him with everything we have. Be careful of what comes out of our mouths; use our hands for only that which is needful and pleases God; do not allow our feet to take us to wrong places; be careful to guard our eyes against looking at things that cause us to lust, to sin, etc. Always remember whose children we are and act accordingly.

> "Flee youthful lusts, but follow righteousness, faith, love, peace, with them that call on the Lord out of a pure heart" (2 Timothy 2:22).

We are to flee lusts. We are to follow righteousness, faith, love, and peace. Notice especially with whom we are to follow these things. It is with those who call on the Lord out of a pure heart. Even though it is not explicitly spelled out, I believe this means we need to be careful in choosing close friends. Don't follow the wrong people or the wrong crowd. The Bible says in 1 Corinthians 15:33: "Be not deceived; evil company corrupts good morals."

> "And what concord hath Christ with Belial? Or what part hath he that believeth with an infidel?... Wherefore, come out from among them, and be ye separate saith the Lord" (2 Corinthians 6:15, 17).

> "Ye adulterer and adulteresses, know ye not that the friendship of the world is enmity with God? Whosoever, therefore, will be a friend of the world is the enemy of God" (James 4:4).

Again, we should be careful in choosing close friends.

Chapter 4
The Holy Spirit

When we become children of God, the Holy Spirit comes to live within us. We are not on our own as we seek to live our lives in obedience to the Lord and His Word. The Holy Spirit will help, enabling us to do this.

> *"And I will pray the Father, and He shall give you another Comforter, that He may abide with you forever"* (John 14:16).

Notice He (Jesus speaking) says He, the Comforter, the Holy Spirit, will abide with us forever.

> *"But the Comforter, which is the Holy Ghost, whom the Father will send in my name, He shall teach you all things"* (John 14:26a).

The Holy Spirit teaches us as we read and study the Word. The more we read, and the more we obey, the more we learn.

> *"Likewise the Spirit also helpeth our infirmities; for we know not what we should pray for as we ought; but the Spirit itself maketh intercession for us with groanings that cannot be uttered. And He that searches the hearts knoweth what is the mind of the Spirit, because He maketh intercession for the saints according to the will of God"* (Romans 8:26-27).

The Holy Spirit helps us in our weakness, etc., and He prays for us. When we do not know how to pray, He does and intercedes for us. How blessed we are in this truth.

> "Now we have received not the Spirit of the world, but the Spirit which is of God; that we might know the things that are freely given to us of God. Which things also we speak, not in the words that man's wisdom teacheth, but which the Holy Ghost teacheth; comparing spiritual things with spiritual" (1 Corinthians 2:12-13).

God has given us His Spirit so we can know the things He has freely given to us. And again, we see the Holy Spirit teaches as we seek to learn and to know Him.

2 Corinthians 3:17 tells us the Lord is that Spirit. God the Father, God the Son, and God the Holy Spirit—all involved with you and me.

> "Now He which establisheth us with you in Christ, and hath anointed us, is God; Who hath also sealed us, and given us the earnest of the Spirit in our hearts" (2 Corinthians 11-22).

Could we be any more blessed? Does this not stir our hearts to praise and worship Him who loves us so much? He has established us, anointed us, sealed us, and given us His Spirit.

> "He hath shewed thee, O man, what is good; and what doth the Lord require of thee, but to do justly, and to love mercy, and to walk humbly with our God" (Micah 6:8).

He has given us all that is required for us to do just that. May we walk worthy.

> "Nevertheless, I tell you the truth, it is expedient for you that I go away; for if I go not away, the Comforter will not come unto you; but if I depart, I will send him unto you. And when He is come, He will reprove the world of sin, and of righteousness, and of judgment; of sin because they believe not in me...Howbeit when He, the Spirit of truth is come, He will guide you into all truth;

for He shall not speak of himself; but whatsoever He shall hear, that shall He speak; and He will show you things to come" (John 16:7-9, 13-14).

The Holy Spirit reproves of sin, righteousness, and judgment. He also guides us into all truth as we study the Bible and as we are submitted to Him. May we always be sensitive and obedient to His leading.

"In whom also after ye believed, ye were sealed with that Holy Spirit of promise" (Ephesians 1:13b).

We are sealed by the Holy Spirit. Can anyone break that seal or annul what God has done? No, we are secure in and by Him and in the Holy Spirit.

"That He would grant you, according to the riches of his glory, to be strengthened with might by his Spirit in the inner man" (Ephesians 3:16).

The Holy Spirit strengthens us. He strengthens us with might! What a great promise and, also, a great prayer for us or for someone else who is going through difficult times.

Chapter 5
SIN HAS CONSEQUENCES

Sin has consequences for those who trust in God as well as those who do not. Satan would love for us to think that is not true. He presents sin as something beautiful that we will like and enjoy. He never shows us the downside or the real truth.

It started in the Garden of Eden when he tempted Eve. He lied to her. He told her it was not true when God said they would die if they ate of the fruit of the tree of life. Satan said, "You shall surely not die." She succumbed to his temptation, thinking, "the tree was good for food; that it was pleasant to the eyes; and a tree to be desired to make one wise." We know how that turned out, don't we? What had seemed to be good, what she thought was pleasant to the eyes, and what she thought was to be desired, turned out to be quite different than it had seemed.

When it was too late, after she and Adam both sinned by eating the fruit, the realization of the truth came. Sin entered, and both of them suffered the consequences of their actions and sin. We still suffer from those consequences today. We would do well to remember Eve's thoughts and the consequences of those actions when we are tempted to sin against God. It may look okay or even good in some ways, but the end result will definitely be anything but good. We would do well to remember Adam when someone close to us encourages us to act in disobedience to God, as Eve did to him.

"For whom the Lord loveth He chastens and

scourgeth every son whom He receiveth. If ye endure chastening, God dealeth with you as with sons; for what son is he whom He chasteneth not?" (Hebrews 12:6-7).

Hebrews goes on to say that chastening is for our own profit, so that we can be partakers of His holiness. When we sin, it affects our relationship and our fellowship with God until we confess and turn from it. There is no greater joy than unbroken fellowship with our Lord and Savior. Sin may 'feel' good for a short while, but the day of reckoning will come. That short time of 'feel good' is nothing compared to walking in fellowship and obedience to Him. Do we really think that sin is worth losing that? Is it worth the temporary loss of the peace, the joy, and the fulfillment that comes from knowing and walking in obedience to Him? If we truly love Him, is it worth grieving the Holy Spirit? Is it worth the consequences? If we could ask Eve and Adam if it was worth the consequences, what do you think their answer would be?

Moses was a man of God chosen by God to lead His people out of Egypt. In Numbers 20:12, we read where God told him he would not be allowed to go into the promised land because of his disobedience (God had told him to speak to the rock for water, but instead of speaking, he struck the rock instead). Sin and disobedience have consequences.

In Numbers 32:9-13, Israel was now ready to go into the promised land that God had given them. They were to go in and take it. But they became afraid — not trusting God — and became discouraged from going in as the Lord had commanded. As a result, the Lord's anger was kindled against them. God made them wander in the wilderness for forty years. *Sin has consequences*. Despite those consequences of their sin, God never left them during those forty years. In Exodus 13:21-22, we read that He went before them in a pillar of cloud by day and was with them as a pillar of fire at night.

David is said to be a man after God's own heart. However, because of his sin, God said the sword would never depart from his house.

> *"Now, therefore, the sword shall never depart from your house because thou have despised me, and taken the wife of Uriah, the Hittite, to be thy wife"* (2 Samuel 12:10).

The following shows some of the things that happened as a result. 2 Samuel 13 tells us of David's son, Amnon, who raped his half-sister, Tamar. Absalom's (Tamar's brother) servants then murdered Amnon. David and Absalom's relationship failed. Then, Absalom was killed in a battle between them and their followers (2 Samuel 18). These and many more things resulted from their failure to believe and obey God. David did repent, but the consequences of sin were still there.

The Bible tells us in Galatians 6:7: "Be not deceived; God is not mocked, for whatsoever a man soweth, that shall he also reap." Let us be careful of the kind of seed we sow. Sow seeds of unbelief and disobedience, and reaping will surely come. *Sin has consequences*. Sow seeds of love, worship, obedience, kindness, etc., and reap those consequences. Which reaping sounds better to you? No contest, right? Galatians 6:9 says, "And let us not be weary in well-doing, for in due season we shall reap, if we faint not." In due season, we will harvest crops of love, worship, obedience, and kindness. Instead of being penitent for sowing the wrong seed, we can thank and praise God for His Word and His Spirit in leading us to sow 'good' seed.

Chapter 6
PRAYER

> *"And I looked for a man among them, that they should make up a hedge, and stand in the gap before me for the land, so I would not destroy it, but I found none"* (Ezekiel 22:30).

This is, to me, one of the saddest verses in the Bible. God is speaking of Israel, His chosen people, who have gone so far away from Him that none are praying or 'standing in the gap' for healing and revival. None are praying for the people. What a sad and heartbreaking situation! Let us think about this and see if we can bring it home in a couple of ways.

First, I believe our missionaries are standing in the gap in a very real sense as they take the gospel of the Lord Jesus Christ to others. I am certain they not only share the good news of salvation through Jesus Christ, but they also pray for those who do not know Him. In other words, they stand in the gap between the unsaved and God with their prayers and with their witness. You and I also have the opportunity to stand in the gap by lifting up our missionaries in prayer as they serve at home and in foreign lands. We can pray:

- For them to remain strong in their faith and commitment to God
- For them to remain faithful to His calling upon their hearts and lives
- For His protection and provision for them

- That He would use them and their witness to turn hearts to Jesus Christ as they share the gospel
- That He would encourage them
- That He would bless them and their ministry
- That all would be done for His honor and glory.

To bring it even closer to home, who is on your prayer list? Think about this for a moment. Is there someone you know whom God has brought into your life, or someone in your family for whom you need to stand in the gap on their behalf? Surely each of us knows at least one person, and I dare say more than one, who needs our prayers. Are we standing in the gap for those persons, or is God still looking for someone to pray for them? Is He having to say, "I found none"?

Often, I hear this remark: "There is no point in praying for him or her. It is hopeless." How much faith is in that statement? Is there any at all? Absolutely none! Do you know someone that you have given up on and tossed aside? Is there someone you have declared hopeless? If so, I pray you will come to exercise faith and realize it is never hopeless. As long as there is breath, there is and should be hope. There should always be faith and hope in our great and loving God, with whom the Bible tells us nothing is impossible. The problem comes when we have our eyes on the person when we should be looking at our God, who "is not willing that any should perish, but that all would come to repentance."

Also, the Bible tells us in Luke 18:1: "...that men ought always to pray and not to faint." Don't faint or grow weary. I have to admit there have been times when I was beginning to grow weary. When that happens, we can turn to God with a simple prayer: *God, help me not to become weary. Help me persevere and continue to pray or to do, whichever is the situation.* God will answer that prayer. Isaiah 40:29 reads, "He giveth power to the faint; and to those who have no might He increaseth strength." Isaiah 40:31 says, "But they that wait upon the Lord shall renew their strength; they shall mount up with wings as eagles; they shall run, and not be weary; and they shall walk, and not faint." You see, God has a Word (scripture) that is living, that can meet our every need and more. He never fails.

Have you ever begun to pray for someone or a situation and don't really know how to pray? Take comfort in Romans 8:26-27:

> *"Likewise, the Spirit also helpeth our infirmity; for we know not what we should pray for as we ought; but the Spirit himself maketh intercession for us with groanings which cannot be uttered. And He that searcheth the hearts knoweth what is the need of the Spirit, because He maketh intercession for the saints."*

Be thankful that when we do not know how to pray, God knows. Thank Him that the Holy Spirit within us takes those prayers and intercedes for us. If our prayers need 'cleaning' or clarifying, He takes care of it for us. God is always with us. Through the Holy Spirit, whom He has given to us, we have all we ever need for any situation.

I once prayed for something for six or seven years. I'm not sure I had any more faith than a grain of mustard seed. During those years, I would look at the situation and say, "There is no way this will ever happen." At the same time, I thought that God could make it happen if it were His will. So, I continued to pray. And God answered my prayer after all those years of praying. It happened at just the right time. His timing was absolutely perfect. As for the doubts, they came when my eyes were on the situation, and not on our God, with whom nothing is impossible. So, may we keep praying, and as we do, keep our eyes on Him and not on the situation. We look to Him in faith and for His will to be done.

In Isaiah 41:14, we read: "Produce your cause, saith the Lord; bring forth your strong reasons, saith the king of Jacob." This is an invitation to lay our case before God as we come to Him in prayer. How blessed we are in God who loves us so much, and who invites us to come in prayer and faith before Him? He invites us to bring our requests and to 'argue' the reason for our requests.

We are actually encouraged in scripture to persist in our prayers. Isaiah 62:6-7 explains:

> *"I have set watchmen upon thy walls, O Jerusalem, who shall never hold their peace day nor night; ye that make mention of the Lord, keep not silence, and give him no rest, till He establish, and till He make Jerusalem a praise in the earth."*

If we pray in God's will, the principle here is to give Him no rest until we receive the answer. With promises like this, we should never grow weary. We know that in His perfect time, God will answer.

My challenge is for us to always stand in the gap for our missionaries and all those God brings into our lives. May He never look at one of our loved ones, or someone we know who is not a Christian, and say there was no one standing in the gap, that there was no one praying for them.

I pray that we would remember to lift in prayer those that serve in all branches of our military. Pray especially for those who are not God's children, that their hearts might be opened to put their faith in Jesus Christ and be saved. Pray that God will protect, strengthen, sustain, encourage, and comfort them. May we also pray this same comfort, strength, and encouragement for their families.

Years ago, God gave me this scripture that I pray for myself, my daughter, Lisa, my granddaughters, Rachel and Anna, and for my great-granddaughter, Riley. It is Deuteronomy 30:6:

> *"And the Lord thy God will circumcise thy heart and the heart of thy seed, to love the Lord thy God with all thine heart and with all thy soul, that thou mayest live."*

This is a promise; the beautiful part of it is that, as in any prayer, it lives on after one dies. It not only covers me and my descendants (seed) that are a part of me now, but it covers those who will come even after I have left this world. It covers all my seed. This is such a comfort. God has given us a promise and a way to pray for those who come after us. What a loving God we serve!

Another promise is found in Isaiah 44:3: "For I will pour water upon him that is thirsty, and floods upon his dry ground; I will pour my Spirit upon thy seed, and my blessing upon thine offspring." Look for His promises, such as this, in His Word. Claim it, for He invites us to do so. He says in Isaiah 43:26 for us to "put him in remembrance; let us plead together."

His promises can give us such peace. When God says it, we know it is real. When He promises, it will most surely come in His way and in His time. It may or may not come in our lifetime, but God's promises are true and never fail.

I had a cousin who lived his life apart from God. I know his parents and others prayed for him over many years. Both of his parents died like so many in Hebrews 11, never receiving the answer to their prayers. But in the last years of my cousin's life, all those prayers were answered. He was saved by the grace of God through Jesus Christ. You see, our prayers don't die when we do. God never *ever* forgets. He is always faithful.

Joshua 23:14 reads:

> *"And behold, this day, I am going the way of all the earth; and ye know in all your hearts and in all your souls, that not one thing hath failed of all the good things which the Lord your God spoke concerning you; all are come to pass unto you, and not one thing hath failed thereof."*

Joshua 21:45 says:

> *"There failed nothing of any good thing which the Lord had spoken unto the house of Israel; all came to pass."*

God's faithfulness is seen here in these verses. His faithfulness has not changed. It is still perfect today and always.

Here is another promise concerning our children and grandchildren, etc.

> *"As for me, this is my covenant with them, saith the Lord: My Spirit that is upon thee, and my Words which I have put in thy mouth, shall not depart out of thy mouth, nor out of the mouth of thy seed, nor out of the mouth of thy seed's seed, saith the Lord, from henceforth and forever"* (Isaiah 59:21).

In this verse, He is speaking of Zion and Jacob, but I believe it applies to all of us who are God's children. We are told in Galatians 3:28 that "there is neither Jew nor Gentile, male nor female, but we are all one in Christ Jesus."

He has taught me to pray scripture, and here are some I've chosen. I can pray for those here now and those to come. Ephesians 1:15-19 reads:

> *"[I] cease not to give thanks for you, making mention of you in my prayers; that the God of our Lord Jesus Christ, the Father of glory, may give unto you the spirit of wisdom and revelation in the knowledge of him, the eyes of your understanding being enlightened, that you may know what is the hope of his calling, and what the riches of the glory of his inheritance in the saints, and what is the exceeding greatness of his power toward us who believe, according to the working of his mighty power."*

This is a powerful prayer to pray for ourselves and those we love.

Philippians 1:9-11 is another wonderful prayer straight from the Word of God:

> *"And this I pray, that your love may abound yet more and more in knowledge and in all judgment;*

> *that ye may approve things that are excellent; that ye may be sincere and without offense till the day of Christ, being filled with the fruits of righteousness, which are by Christ Jesus, unto the glory and praise of God."*

What better way to pray than to pray God's Word for us and for others?

Another wonderful prayer from Ephesians 3:14-19:

> *"For this cause I bow my knees unto the Father of our Lord Jesus Christ, of whom the whole body of heaven and earth Is named, that He would grant you, according to the riches of his glory, to be strengthened with might by his Spirit in the inner man; that Christ may dwell in your hearts by faith; that ye, being rooted and grounded in love, may be able to comprehend with all saints, what is the breadth, and length, and depth, and height, and to know the love of Christ, which passeth knowledge, that ye might be filled with the fullness of God."*

This is another beautiful and meaningful prayer that can be prayed for anyone on our prayer lists. Colossians 1:9-12:

> *"For this cause, we also, since the day we heard it, do not cease to pray for you, and to desire that ye might be filled with the knowledge of his will in all wisdom and spiritual understanding; that ye might walk worthy of the Lord unto all pleasing, being faithful in every good work, and increasing in the knowledge of God; strengthened with all might, according to his glorious power, unto all patience and long-suffering with joyfulness; giving thanks unto the Father, who hath made us fit to be partakers of the inheritance of the saints in light."*

Think about the words of these prayers. Hear these beautiful requests that we can pray for one another.

These are a few of the examples of praying scripture over our loved ones and for ourselves. There are, of course, many more scriptures we can use in praying. God's Word abounds in so many spiritual riches and truths for us.

We need to heed 2 Chronicles 7:14:

> *"If my people, who are called by name, shall humble themselves and pray, and seek my face, and turn from our wicked ways, then will I hear from heaven, and will forgive their sin, and will heal their land."*

So often, I hear people refer to this, and they assume it means to pray for our leaders and those who do not know Jesus Christ. We certainly should pray for them, but that is not what the verse says. It speaks to those of us who know Jesus Christ; that we need to walk in obedience to Him and His Word. We need to humble ourselves, pray, seek His face, and turn from any sin that is in our hearts and lives. His promise of forgiveness and healing depends on our obedience to this verse. Let us pray and ask God for repentance in us where needed. Let us pray that we and our brothers and sisters-in-Christ would do the things listed in this verse. Then we can pray for our country's leaders. Then we can pray for others who have not placed their faith in Jesus Christ.

May we pray for our church, the body of Christ. Let us pray for one another "that ye (we) may be blameless and harmless; children of God, without rebuke amid a crooked and perverse nation, among whom ye shine as lights in the world, holding forth the Word of life" (Philippians 2:13-16a).

God's Word is a rich treasure in which we need to 'dig' often. Regardless of how often we 'dig,' there will always be new 'treasure' to be revealed. Let us not neglect to search faithfully.

He has given us this wonderful privilege of prayer. May we communicate with Him often every day. May we pray according to His will. There are some things we know are His will. We can ask that He do those things for His namesake and for His honor and glory. Other times, we may need to add 'if it by thy will' to our prayers, knowing that His will is always best. May we pray not only for ourselves but for others as well. And may He be glorified in all things.

Chapter 7
CLEAVING

So often, when talking to someone about difficulties in life, I remark, "Hold on to the Lord and keep going." So, I began researching scriptures on cleaving to the Lord.

Cleave means *to adhere to or cling to, stick to, or hold fast*. And isn't that what we need to do in times of difficulty? Actually, we need to do it at all times, but especially in those difficult situations. We need to cling to and hold fast to the Lord and His Word.

Sometimes we have a tendency to go to friends or loved ones instead of God. I'm not saying there's anything wrong with that. Friends are wonderful, and we are so blessed to have them to support us and to pray for us. But God is the "friend that sticks closer than a brother." So, we cleave to Him to see us through whatever difficulties come our way. He never fails. He may use some of those friends to walk alongside us. If so, we need to give thanks for them, that they care and are willing to help. He doesn't always make the way easy, but He makes it doable. And He is with us through whatever situations come to us.

He invites us to cleave unto Him. Joshua 23:8 reads, "Cleave unto the Lord your God." Joshua 22:5 says, "But take diligent heed to do the commandments and the law, which Moses, the servant of God charged you; to love the Lord your God, and to walk in all his ways and to keep his commandments; to cleave unto Him; and to serve Him with all your heart and with all your soul." Cleave unto Him by being obedient to Him and His Word.

> *"Who, when he came and had seen the grace of God, was glad and exhorted them all, that with purpose of heart, they would cleave/cling unto the Lord"* (Acts 11:23).

To cleave unto the Lord, we must walk with Him, which means to walk in obedience to Him and His Word. If we are not doing this, fellowship is broken. But confession and repentance heal and restore the fellowship, and we can cleave fast to Him. Who better could we have to walk with us through the storm and through each day of our life? He says in Isaiah 41:10, "Fear thou not, for I am with thee. Be not dismayed, for I am thy God; I will strengthen thee; yea, I will uphold thee with the right hand of my righteousness." We need to remember these words. Whatever is happening in our lives, God is with us. He is holding us up.

Isaiah 41:13 says, "For I, the Lord thy God, will hold thy right hand, saying unto thee, fear not, for I will help thee." The Lord thy God—sweet, sweet words. This makes it so personal; the Lord thy God. He holds our hands and helps us. Another wonderful promise.

> *"When thou passeth through the waters, I will be with thee; and through the rivers, they shall not overflow thee; when thou walketh through the fire, thou shalt not be burned, neither shall the flame kindle upon thee"* (Isaiah 43:2).

Whatever is happening in our lives, we need not be afraid. God is with us. He is in control. Even through the water, the rivers, and the fire, He, God Himself, will see that we are not overcome by these things. He will see us through.

> *"And even in your old age, I am He; and even to gray hair, I will carry you; I have made and I will bear; even I will carry and deliver you"* (Isaiah 46:4).

Ah, even in old age and gray hair, we can continue to cleave to Him. He promises to carry and deliver us. We are so blessed with the comfort of this promise from our loving God.

Whenever we walk through the storms of life, we are never alone. Whatever is happening and at whatever age, remember that. We have the God of heaven and earth, the God of all that is therein with us. What a wonderful thought and knowledge that God himself is with us always. He says in Hebrews that He will never leave us nor forsake us. He is our strength and our helper. Psalms 46:1 reads, "God is our refuge and strength; a very present help in trouble." Think on Him and His Word. The Holy Spirit uses the Word to strengthen, sustain, and keep us—to cause us to cleave and hold fast to Him and His Word. We are never, ever alone. We are never, ever without help, and it is the greatest help possible.

> *"Although the fig tree shall not blossom; neither shall fruit be in the vines; the labor of the olive shall fail; and the fields shall yield no food; the flock shall be cut off from the fold; and there shall be no herd in the stall; yet I will rejoice in the Lord; I will joy in the God of my salvation"* (Habakkuk 3:17-18).

This verse says that regardless of what happens, we can choose to rejoice in the Lord. We can find joy in the God of our salvation always and forever. We know Who is in control. We know how it all ends.

God, help us to do this. God, help us to be strong in you, turning our eyes upon you, and as the song says, looking into your face; that the things of this life may grow dim in the light of wonderful, glorious you – your glory and your grace through Jesus Christ, our Lord.

Chapter 8
It is All About God

We are made for the glory of God. Isaiah 43:7a says, "Even everyone who is called by my name; for I have created him for my glory." As His children, our goal should be to know and glorify Him. The thing in life that will give us the most pleasure is to know God and to walk in obedience to Him. It brings more joy, delight, contentment, and peace than anything. It also gives God pleasure. He loves us, and it is always pleasing when we, as His children, walk with Him. If a parent has a child that goes astray, we know the grief it brings to that parent's heart. But if a person has given their heart and life to Jesus Christ and walks with Him, we then know the joy that it brings. So we can understand, at least partially, when the Bible tells us it grieves the Holy Spirit when we sin.

> *"But let them that glorieth glory in this, that he understandeth and knoweth me, that I am the Lord who exerciseth lovingkindness, justice, and righteousness in the earth; for in these things I delight, saith the Lord"* (Jeremiah 9:24).

The greatest, the highest, the best thing that can occupy our minds is God, His name, His nature, His person, His work, His doing, His existence. Contemplating on Him makes a difference in our minds and in our entire beings. 2 Corinthians 3:18 says, "But we all with unveiled face, beholding as in a mirror the glory of the Lord, are changed into the same image from glory to glory, even as by the Spirit of the Lord." Thinking on Him changes us, grows us, and stretches our minds. Thinking on Him and His Word grows us spiritually. We are being changed by the Holy Spirit to become more like Him.

If we desire to lose our sorrows and our cares, we need to lose ourselves in communion (prayer) with God. Sometimes we may need to sit before Him and allow the Spirit to minister to us. He can soothe our pain, our sorrows, our cares. Whatever our problem, He knows. He cares. That knowledge alone will bring comfort. As we sit before Him, we should acknowledge that He knows all about whatever is happening with us. Receive His calmness. Receive His peace. He will handle whatever is troubling us. He will refresh, renew, and invigorate us.

If we, as His children, are to be godly, we must respond to Him in trust and obedience, in faith and worship, in prayer and praise, and in submission and service. This is a life that is pleasing to Him and one that is a blessing to us.

We want to know Him, not just about Him. A little knowledge *of* God is worth more than a lot of knowledge *about* Him. We come to know Him by reading His Word and hearing what He says. We come to know Him by walking with Him in obedience to His word. We come to know Him by praying to Him and being filled with the Holy Spirit.

1 Corinthians 10:31 reminds us that "Whether, therefore, ye eat or drink, or whatever ye do, do all to the glory of God." We need to listen carefully to this verse. Whatever we do, it should always be to the glory of God. Perhaps we should examine ourselves before doing some things, especially if they are questionable. We should ask the question: *Am I doing this for the glory of God?* If not, then we should probably reconsider and make it a matter of prayer, seeking God's will before proceeding.

Psalms 50:15 says, "Call upon me in the day of trouble; I will deliver thee, and thou shalt glorify me." Have you ever considered that when we call upon Him for deliverance, it is an opportunity to glorify God? What a blessing that He will not only deliver us, but we shall glorify Him! Thank you, Father!

Psalms 29:2 reads, "Give unto the Lord the glory due unto his name; worship the Lord in the beauty of holiness." How often do we give to the Lord the glory that is His and due to Him? When a prayer is answered, let us give Him all the glory. For all He has given us, for health, homes, family, love, and other things too numerous to name, do we give Him thanks, praise, honor, and glory? May we begin today to do this.

John 14:13 says, "And whatever ye shall ask in my name, that will I do, that the Father may be glorified in the son." First of all, I believe to ask in Jesus name is to ask in accordance with His will, knowing that Jesus would never ask for something outside the will of the Father. His will and the Father's will are always the same. Therefore, I do not believe we can ask for something outside His or the Father's will and expect Him to answer. But this verse tells me when He answers our prayers, it is always for the glory of God.

> *"If any man speak, let him speak as the oracles of God; if any man minister, let him do it as the ability which God giveth, that God in all things may be glorified through Jesus Christ, to whom be praise and dominion forever and ever. Amen"* (1 Peter 4:11).

Have you ever heard a wealthy person say they made their money all by themselves? They may say they did it through their intelligence and their hard work. They do not realize who gave them all that intelligence and ability. Whatever we do or say, whatever we have, we are to acknowledge that the wherewithal, the means, and the ability all come from the Lord. All the praise and glory belong to Him.

Psalms 96:8 says, "Give unto the Lord the glory due unto his name, bring an offering and come into his courts." Whatever we say or do, it is to be to the glory of God. It is only through Him and in Him that we can say or do anything; so where does all the glory belong? It belongs to Him and Him alone. When we bring our offering, it is from that which God has given us. When we serve in any way, it is through the health and strength that God gives us. It is all about Him, His goodness, His grace to us that we may serve Him and others.

> *"And upon a set day Herod, arrayed in royal apparel, sat upon his throne, and made an oration unto them (Tyre and Sidon). And the people gave a shout, saying, it is the voice of a god and not of a man. And immediately an angel of the Lord smote him, because he gave not God the glory; and he was eaten of worms, and died"* (Acts 12:21-23).

Let us always be certain and faithful to ascribe all glory and honor to the Lord our God. May we never take for ourselves that which belongs to Him.

"That at the knee of Jesus every knee should bow, of things in heaven, and things in earth, and things under the earth, and that every tongue should confess that Jesus Christ is Lord, to the glory of God, the Father" (Philippians 2:10-11).

What a day that will be! Everything and everyone will confess that Jesus Christ is Lord. It will all be to the glory of our Lord and our God.

1 Chronicles 16:8 reads, "Give thanks unto the Lord, call upon his name and make known his deeds among the people." As we give thanks and call upon Him, may we tell others of the wonderful things He has done, being careful to always give the glory to Him. 1 Chronicles 16:29 says, "Give unto the Lord the glory due unto his name; bring an offering and come before him; worship the Lord in the beauty of his holiness." May we always give God all the glory due to His holy name. May we worship Him as we give our offerings in thanksgiving and praise to Him and all He has given us.

As we contemplate God's greatness and glory, we shall undoubtedly be humbled by our own insignificance and sinfulness. But yet, we are comforted by His great love for us and by the unsearchable riches of His mercy shown through Jesus Christ.

As our knowledge of God increases, so does our strength, our endurance, our peace, and our joy. Knowing Him makes a difference when we experience grief, disappointment, or trials of any kind. We are not overcome by them. Instead, we are overcomers through Him that loves us. We "can do all things through God who strengthens us." He may not always make the way easy, but He is always faithful to see us through. To Him be all glory, praise, and honor.

Chapter 9
Soothing Balm

"And we know that all things work together for good to them that love God; to them who are the called according to his purpose" (Romans 8:28).

God has used this verse so many times in my life to sustain my faith, to encourage me, and to keep me going. It tells us that all things, good or bad, He will work for our good. Only God can do that. Only God can take a bad thing and work it for good, because nothing is impossible with Him.

When you're in a difficult or painful situation, think on this scripture. Remember that as painful or difficult it may be, it is somehow working for our good. We may not be able to see how, but God is faithful. We can trust Him to do what He says. The knowledge of that helps and makes it easier to bear. It is like rubbing salve or ointment on a wound. The wound is still there, but the salve or ointment is soothing. It is also healing. We may not see the healing right away, but you know it is happening. God knows all about whatever occurs in our lives, and He cares. Somehow, He is working good out of it.

He also uses this verse to change our attitude in these situations. If we must have difficulties and painful situations, it is wonderful to know He is working them for our good. As a result, amid these things, we can thank Him for His work in it. We can praise Him that He is our God who will work and bring good out of any circumstances. It should be of comfort for us to know that. We find soothing for our troubled soul in Him and the truth of His Word.

Another scripture that helps during these times is Proverbs 3:5: "Trust in the Lord with all your heart and lean not to your understanding." This scripture informs us that we will not always understand why something is happening in our lives. When we do not know why, we are to trust in Him with all our hearts. When we do not understand, we can, by an act of our will, continue to trust in Him. This makes all the difference in the world; just learning to trust Him with all our heart. I have found God does not always change our situations so much as He changes us and our attitude in them.

This can make such a difference in our lives. Instead of being frustrated, afraid, or angry, God will give us an attitude of faith, an attitude that trusts He is working good and that He will see us through whatever is taking place. Instead of complaining, we receive from Him a heart of thanksgiving and a prayer that, somehow, He will be glorified.

The Holy Spirit is always here to turn our thoughts back to God and His Word, to change our complaints to thanks and praise, and to change our wrong attitude or whatever sin is present at the time. He will do this if we are sensitive and obedient to Him and His prompting.

Psalms 55:22 urges us to "Cast thy burden upon the Lord, and He shall sustain thee, He shall never suffer the righteous to be moved." This is another invitation from our Lord. We can cast our burden upon Him. We can trust Him to carry and sustain us through whatever comes our way as we look to Him in faith. Psalms 56:3-4 says, "When I am afraid, I will trust in thee. In God I will praise his Word, in God I have put my trust; I will not fear what flesh can do unto me." Remember that. When fear comes, remember to trust in Him, praise Him, and let Him take the fear away.

Psalms 57:1 reads, "Be merciful unto me, O God, be merciful unto me; for my soul trusteth in thee, yea in the shadow of thy wings will I make my refuge, until these calamities be passed by." When we are in a difficult or painful situation, what better place to be than in the shadow of His wings? There is none. We are safe in Him as we make Him our refuge.

> *"Because he hath set his love upon me, therefore will I deliver him; I will set him on high, because he hath known my name. He shall call upon me, and I will answer him, I will be with him in trouble; I will deliver him and honor him"* **(Psalm 91:14-14).**

This, too, is a soothing balm for a troubled soul or difficult times. He will be with us and deliver us. He also says He will honor us. Can one imagine? Almighty God himself will honor us. Of all people, we are most blessed.

We may not always be certain what life holds for us. But one thing we can always be certain of, and that is God and His Word. We can be sure He holds us. Isaiah 41:13a says, "For I, the Lord thy God will hold thy right hand." We can be sure of His faithfulness to us. He loved us enough to send His son, Jesus, to die for our sins. He raised Him from the dead on the third day that we might have new life in Him. He received Him back into heaven and gave us the gift of the Holy Spirit, who lives within those of us who are His children. As it states in Acts 17:28: "In him, we live and move and have our being ..."

Romans 8:28 is a balm that can soothe the soul. We can be certain that, because He said so, all things work together for our good if we love Him and are His children. We can know that trusting in Him with all our heart is far better than leaning to our own understanding. We can be confident His Word will never fail. He will never fail. God's Word is a soothing balm for the soul.

Chapter 10
GIVING

> *"And, he (Jesus) looked up and saw the rich men casting their gifts into the treasury. And he also saw a certain poor widow casting in two mites. And he said, of a truth, I tell you that this poor widow has cast in more than them all. For all of these have given out of their abundance, but she, out of her poverty, has cast in all the living that she had"* (Luke 21:1-4).

Probably not many of us sacrifice to give to the Lord as much as this widow. I dare say most of us fit in that first category — giving out of our abundance, the abundance which God has given us. I am not saying there is anything wrong with giving out of our abundance. We certainly should give of that which God has given to us. However, we need to make sure that we are giving according to God's will and not our own.

> *"Honor the Lord with thy substance, and with the first fruits of all thine increase; so shall thy barns be filled with plenty"* (Proverbs 3:9-10).

> *"The first of the first fruits of thy land thou shalt bring into the house of the Lord thy God"* (Exodus 23:19a).

We are to give Him the first fruits. That tells us we are to give to God first and foremost –with our first fruits to Him before anything else.

> *"Bring all the tithes into the storehouse, that there might be food in my house, and test me now herewith, saith the Lord of hosts, if I will not open for you the windows of heaven, and pour out for you a blessing, that there shall not be room enough to receive it"* (Malachi 3:10).

We can never out-give the Lord. Although, I pray that when we give, we are motivated by love for Him and obedience to His Word, and not just for what we will receive in return. Then when we are blessed by Him in our giving, may we give Him all the glory and praise with thanksgiving.

> *"But this I say, he who soweth sparingly shall also reap sparingly; and he who soweth bountifully shall reap bountifully. Every man according as he purposeth in his heart, so let Him give; not grudgingly or of necessity, for God loveth a cheerful giver"* (2 Corinthians 9:6-7).

God wants us to give cheerfully. We should give with a heart of gratitude to God, who loves us so much. We should give with thanksgiving, realizing that He is the one who gives us the means to give, recognizing that all we have comes from Him. James 1:17 says, "Every good and every perfect gift is from above and cometh down from the Father of lights." He wants us to give because we love Him and because we want to and not because we feel we have to.

How many of us decide how much we are going to give without praying and seeking God's direction and will? Then, once we have given whatever amount we decided on for that period, do we close off the giving until next period, regardless of whatever needs are brought to our attention? Do you know why Ephesians 4:28 admonishes us to work? "Let him that stole steal no more. but rather let him labor, working with his hands the thing that is good, that he may have to give to him that needeth." That is a different perspective than we normally think of, isn't it? He says we work to be able to help others, to give to those who are in need. We are not working just for ourselves, but also for others. 1 John 3:17 says, "But whoso hath this world's good, and seeth his brother have need, and shutteth up his bowels of compassion from him, how dwelleth the love of God in him?" We are to show love and compassion on those less fortunate than we are, by responding to needs that God brings to our attention.

Proverbs 19:17 reads, "He that hath pity upon the poor lendeth unto the Lord, and that which he hath given will he pay him again." A promise is in this verse. God is saying whatever we give is as unto Him and will be given back to us. But again, we need to be sure 'getting it back' is not our motive for giving. May we give out of love for our Lord and love for others.

> **"Lend, hoping for nothing again; and your reward shall be great, and ye shall be the sons of the Highest; for he is kind to the unthankful and to the evil" (Luke 6:35b).**

Ouch! Can we do that? Have you ever loaned to someone and, in the end, you 'write it off'? If there is a great need there, would we do that? It is what God is saying we should do. We are to have pity upon the poor. It will be as if we were lending unto God.

Remember the boy on the mount in John chapter 6? A great multitude had followed Jesus up the mountain, where He sat with His disciples. The boy had five loaves of bread and two small fish. The Bible doesn't tell us, but apparently, he freely gave what he had. That is a testimony within itself. Hear the lesson we need to learn from that selfless giving. As long as the bread and fish remained with him, they were just that – five loaves of bread and two small fish. But when he gave them to Jesus, he was fed, and they also fed a multitude of people.

"And they did all eat and were filled; and they took up of the fragments that remained twelve baskets full. And they that had eaten were about five thousand men, besides women and children" (Matthew 14:20-21).

What a lesson for us to 'give it away' as God leads. God will multiply our giving in ways we cannot imagine. May we be faithful to give, with thanksgiving, as He leads.

Chapter 11
VICTORY

> *"For we wrestle not against flesh and blood, but against principalities, against powers, against the rulers of the darkness of this world, against spiritual wickedness in high places"* (Ephesians 6:12).

We need to recognize our enemy—the one who would love to cause us to stumble. Ephesians 6:10-11 tell us the only way we can win: "Finally, my brethren, be strong in the Lord, and in the power of his might. Put on the whole armor of God; that ye may be able to stand against the wiles of the devil." We look to God who will give us strength to stand, strength to resist. The Bible says in James 4:7, "Submit yourselves, therefore, to God. Resist the devil and he will flee from you." Don't just stand there—fight! Verses 13-18 in Ephesians 6 give us further instructions for victory:

> *"Wherefore, take unto you the whole armor of God, that ye may be able to withstand in the evil day, and having done all, to stand. Stand, therefore, having your loins girded about with truth, and having on the breastplate of righteousness, and your feet shod with the preparation of the gospel of peace; above all taking the shield of faith, with which ye shall be able to quench all the fiery darts of the wicked. And take the helmet of salvation, and the sword of the Spirit, which is*

> *the Word of God; praying always with all prayer and supplication in the Spirit, and watching thereunto with all perseverance, and supplication for all saints."*

As children of God through Jesus Christ, we should know whom we are fighting. God wants us to know and tells us in Ephesians 6:12. We fight against powers, rulers of darkness, and spiritual wickedness. Then He gives us the way we can win the battle. We cannot win in our own strength, but only in His power and might. All the armor He describes comes from Him. If we want to be girded with truth, we need to know His Word, read it, study it, and be filled with the knowledge of Him and that Word. He and His Word are truth. Faith is the water that puts out the fires of doubt and fear that come from Satan. Our faith is strengthened as we know Him and His Word. The sword is also the Word. When Jesus was tempted by Satan, He used the sword of the Spirit in the same way we should do. He answered Satan with words from the Bible. He used scripture to answer and to rebuke Satan's temptation.

Paul and Silas are in prison. Let's see what happens:

> **"And at midnight Paul and Silas prayed, and sang praises unto God"** (Acts 16:25a).

They are in prison for serving and preaching Jesus Christ. What would our attitude be in this situation? Would we be singing and praising God? Or would we be complaining to God, saying, "Lord, we were obeying you. Now you have let this happen to us. Why?" How could they sing and praise God in prison?

For one thing, they apparently recognized God's sovereignty. They understood that nothing could come to them unless God either willed it or allowed it. That is why they could sing and praise Him. They trusted Him to somehow use it for His honor and glory, and that He would work good out of it. And God did just that. An earthquake came, and all the doors of the prison were opened. Acts 16:30-31 tells us the keeper of the prison fell down before Paul and Silas, asking "Sirs, what must I do to be saved? And they said, Believe on the Lord Jesus Christ, and thou shalt be saved, and thy house. And they spoke unto to him the Word of the Lord, and to all that were in his house." He and all of his family were baptized that very night, and verse 34 says, "he rejoiced, believing in God with all his house." Is this a lesson for us? Paul and Silas left that jail victorious. They had victory over the flesh by their attitude in a difficult situation. Regardless of the circumstances, they chose to thank and praise God. As a result, God used them and that trial to bring sinners home to Jesus Christ. Never underestimate the power of our God.

Studying and knowing scripture is one of the most important things we can do; yet, so often we neglect it. If we want to stand in the day of temptation, we need to know the Word and the author of the Word. Then we can put our faith to stand in God, and not in ourselves. In ourselves, we are helpless against Satan and his forces. But, with God, the victory is ours. How do we know? Because He tells us in 1 John 4:4b: "Greater is He that is in you than he that is in the world."

Chapter 12
AGAPE LOVE

We are commanded in scripture to love others. We are to love them unconditionally, in much the same way that God loves us. His love for us is unconditional. The Bible says He loved us while we were still sinners. Would God tell you to do something you cannot do? Can you make yourself 'feel' love for another person? No, of course not. When He tells us to love our enemies, He is telling us to *agape love* them. *Agape love* is not necessarily an emotional love, but more an act of the will. We cannot do this on our own, but through the power of the Holy Spirit, as we are willing to be obedient to God. We decide to love someone through our actions, regardless of how they treat us. When we decide to obey God in this, the Holy Spirit enables us to do so.

God doesn't say love them only if they treat you well. He doesn't give us an *out* if they treat us badly or if they have a bad attitude and are not very lovable. God loves us, even when, by our actions, we are not very lovable. We are to extend some of that same grace to others that God has extended to us. In doing this and allowing the Holy Spirit to work in us, we become more of the person God wants us to be.

Matthew 22:39 says, "…thou shall love your neighbor as yourself." This is also stated in Leviticus 19:18: "Thou shalt not avenge or bear any grudge against the children of thy people, but thou shalt love thy neighbor as thyself. I am the Lord." What does that mean? Romans 13:10a tells us, "Love worketh no ill to its neighbor." It means we will not harm them, just as we would never deliberately harm ourselves. It means we should not hold on to resentment against them for something they said or did. It means we should not try to get back at them or seek to make them pay for some offense against us, real or supposed.

It means we do unto them as we would have them do unto us. We treat them the way we would like to be treated—loving them in and by our actions.

Matthew 5:44 reads, "But I say unto you, love your enemies; bless them that curse you; do good to them that hate you; and pray for those who despitefully use you." Wow! It gets more difficult, doesn't it? How on earth can we do this? First, we need to see that it is not a commandment to feel something. It is a commandment to do something. It says to bless, do good, and pray for them. Ah, I can do that; not on my own, but because the Holy Spirit will enable me. I can choose to do it in obedience to Him.

John 15:12 states, "This is my commandment, that ye love one another, as I have loved you." How did He love us? He loved us by giving of himself. He loved us by giving His life on the cross of Calvary that we might have life. He gave His all. How much are we willing to give in love for others? Matthew 22:37-39 says, "Jesus said unto him, Thou shalt love the Lord thy God, with all thy heart, and with all thy soul, and with all thy mind. This is the first and great commandment. And the second is like unto it, Thou shalt love thy neighbor as thyself." If we truly love God and have given Him His rightful place in our hearts and lives, then we will want to choose to love others as He loves us. We will desire to do this to obey and please Him. He is, or should be, our first priority in all things. He has given us all we need to be, all that He would have us be, and will do all that He would have us do. We have Him, His Word, and the Holy Spirit abiding in us. He and His grace are sufficient for our every need.

Matthew 27:39 speaks of loving your neighbor. This is not

limited to loving the neighbor next door but loving one another wherever and whenever. In the story of the good Samaritan (Luke chapter 10), Jesus explains that the Samaritan was the neighbor who showed mercy to someone he did not know.

Luke 6:32 states, "For if ye love them who love you, what thanks have ye? For sinners also love those who love them." It is easy to love those who love us and treat us well. Jesus tells us that even sinners do that. But as God's children, we are to be different. It takes humility and the power of God to love the unlovely. It also takes a willing heart.

Ephesians 5:2 says, "Be ye, therefore, followers of Christ, as dear children, and walk in love, as Christ loved us, and gave himself for us as an offering and a sacrifice to God for a sweet-smelling savor." Hear what it says. Agape love is a giving of self. Christ did more than just *feel* love for us. He gave himself. To walk in love as He did, we give of ourselves—first to Him and then to others. It is a sacrificial giving of ourselves, of our love to God and others.

Romans 12:17a, 21 states, "Recompense to man evil for evil... Be not overcome by evil, but overcome evil with good." We can do this through the power of the Holy Spirit, or we can become like our enemy. When we retaliate in like manner with them, have we not become like them? More importantly, we have grieved God and the Holy Spirit by our disobedience.

Before we get too overwhelmed with this, let us stop for a minute and realize we will never be perfect at this; at least, not in this life. But as Philippians 3:14 says, we "press toward the mark for the prize of the high calling of God in Christ Jesus." Knowing we are not perfect in our walk doesn't excuse us from seeking to be obedient.

There will be times when we become angry at something someone has said or done. Most of us fall prey to it at some point. But the key to this is to be sensitive to the Holy Spirit, who will convict. When He makes us aware of our sin, we can immediately lift our confession and repentance to God, asking

Him to help us to respond differently and not to act on that emotional response. 1 John 1:9 says, "If we confess our sin, He is faithful and just to forgive our sin and to cleanse us from all unrighteousness." When this happens to me, God reminds me to pray for myself first, allowing Him to work in me and correct my attitude. After my cleansing and forgiveness, I can pray for the target of my anger.

Emotionally, we usually love people if they act the way we want them to. This is not agape love. Remember that agape love is unconditional—not *I love you if you do this*, or *I love you if you don't do that*. Agape love loves regardless. We are not commanded to like what others do, but we are commanded to agape love them. God does not always like everything we do. He certainly does not like it when we sin. Yet He continues to love us and is always ready to forgive and cleanse.

In the parable of the prodigal son, the father gave the son his inheritance, even though he knew the son was likely not going to live the way he wanted him to live. And the son did exactly what the father expected by squandering his inheritance on riotous living. Did this stop his dad from loving him? No, he loved him in spite of this. His love was unconditional.

When his son returned and was repentant, the father did not withhold his love and acceptance. Instead, he loved him so much, he welcomed him with open arms, much the same way God loves us. Even though he strayed, his father's love apparently never ceased nor did his prayers for this wayward son. Luke 15:20 tells us his father saw him when he was yet a great way off. That tells me his father was looking and waiting for his return. I believe God has that much love for us and much, much more—more than we could possibly ever imagine. I believe the picture of this father watching for his son's return and welcoming him with open arms is a picture of God when we, as His children, have strayed and returned to Him. I believe He watches and waits for our repentance. And He always welcomes the opportunity to welcome us back into fellowship with

Him.

What do you think would have happened to this son had the father reacted differently and had not loved him unconditionally? We really don't know, but the streets of many cities could probably give us a clue. Many people have ended up there because of a lack of unconditional love and possibly condemnation by the people who should love them the most. All on the streets are not there because of this. But many are. Someone failed to show them unconditional love, probably failed to hold them up in prayer, failed to show them God's love, and failed to extend to them some of the grace and love that has been extended to you and me. *God, grant that we never fail to love, that we never fail to stand in the gap for someone, especially those in our family. Thank you, God, for loving us.*

This does not mean we condone anyone in their sinful actions. God does not condone sin, although He is always ready to forgive when there are confession and repentance. But we can make known to them in a loving way that we do not condone their sinful actions. We do not support them in this, but we still love them. We pray for them to come to know Jesus Christ as their Savior and Lord, or to walk in obedience to Him, submitting themselves to Him and His Word. Our children, of all people, should know, beyond a shadow of a doubt, that regardless of what they do, we will always love them and pray for them. But, just as the fellowship is broken when sin comes between God and us until there is repentance, so can the fellowship sometimes be strained or broken in families who take a stand against what God has declared sin. But it is up to us to keep the lines of communication open with those that stray, even though we have no part in their sin.

To conclude, those acting under emotional love may reject a person because they do not like the way that person acts or when that person does something to hurt them or make them angry. This is not so with agape love. It is not selective based on personality or perceived bad treatment. It is based on our decision to obey God and the power of God working in us as we submit to Him and His Word. It means that sometimes we lay aside our desires and interests and choose to love. Agape love gives and does not have to receive in return. It is not self-centered, but God-centered first, then centered on others. Agape love, even when it is not returned, loves anyhow. Agape love is the greater love. It is the giving of one's self.

In my notes is this quote: "Love can only be known by the action it prompts."[1]

Are you aware that you can never run out of love? Did you know the more you love, the more you have? The more you give, the more you have? You absolutely cannot ever run out of love. It is an inexhaustible supply from God. So, give it away, and receive the same, or more, back. GIVE IT AWAY!

Will we be perfect in this? I think not. But I believe God honors a willing heart. He knows our weaknesses, but He also sees and knows our hearts. Hopefully, prayerfully, our hearts are 'set like flint' to love, worship, and obey Him.

---

[1] VINE'S EXPOSITORY DICTIONARY OF NT WORDS

Chapter 13
FORGIVENESS

So often, there are broken relationships within families. For whatever reason, they have become angry with one another and no longer have any communication at all. Then one of the family members dies, and there are regrets. They regret not having healed the broken relationship. Some may say, "You always think there is plenty of time." But, suddenly, there is no more time. So, their advice is "Don't ever put off what needs to be said" to heal the relationships. Say it today. We don't have the assurance of tomorrow, or even the rest of the day. Do not delay forgiving and seeking healing in broken relationships.

I have witnessed this with someone who was dying, and they were sorry they had allowed this unforgiveness to continue. They made remarks indicating how sorry they were about the break in fellowship. After many years of no communication, there had been no effort to find out if they were still alive. And, if so, there had been no effort to find out where they might be living. Do we only love someone if they measure up to our ideals or live the way we think we should? Is that truly love? Certainly, it is not unconditional love. If they are drifting into a life of sin, we should not condone their behavior. I understand some sinful lifestyles may cause a 'crack' in relationships and we do not want to become a part of that sin. But, even then, we should let them know we love them, that we pray for them. We should do our best to keep the lines of communication open.

Sometimes, communication breaks down over disagreement. As Christians, we should be able to disagree, but can we disagree in love? Most husbands and wives don't agree on everything but continue to love one another despite their differences. We should have respect for another person's right to disagree with us, just as we have the right to disagree with them. But so often, instead of respecting someone's right to an opinion, a person just wants their opinion to be valid. The result is often anger and resentment toward one another. God wants us to put aside these feelings of anger and resentment and to walk in love for one another. We mentioned earlier that we are not to live or be controlled by our feelings or emotions. We are to live according to God's Word and the leading of the Holy Spirit within us.

Whatever the reason for the broken relationship, it is wrong according to God's Word. Ephesians 4:32 says:

> *"And grieve not the Holy Spirit of God, whereby ye are sealed unto the day of redemption. Let all bitterness, and wrath, and clamor, and evil speaking, be put away from you, with all malice. And be ye kind one to another, and forgiving one another, even as God, for Christ's sake has forgiven you."*

Also, Colossians 3:13 says, "Forbearing one another, and forgiving one another; if any man has a quarrel against any. Even as Christ forgave you, so also do you." We are to forgive others, always, and at all times for all things, just as Christ has forgiven us.

Years ago, I heard someone say, "I want to forgive the way I want to be forgiven. I want to be completely forgiven, so I need to completely forgive." Even if something is done to hurt us, we need to completely forgive. The Bible says in Romans 5:8 that God forgave us while we were still sinners. When we are and have been forgiven so much, how can we not also forgive others?

Do you remember the attitude of forgiveness demonstrated

by Jesus when He was being crucified? As He hung on that cross, He said: "Father, forgive them." God, grant that we would choose to do the same in forgiving others. May we not withhold from others that which is given to us so freely.

So much of the Christian life is choices. We make them every day. We decide to obey God or to disobey; to love or not to love; to forgive or not to forgive. God loves us in spite of all this. He does not love our sinful actions, but He still loves us. And He always forgives when we confess and repent.

Forgiveness does not necessarily mean we like what someone did or said to hurt us or make us angry. We certainly won't like it if it was wrong. But it does mean we give up the anger and resentment. We give up the desire to punish or get back at them. We choose to forgive them, and we learn not to allow our minds to dwell on the wrong done to us. When we do this, we have the power of the Holy Spirit to help us. We are not left alone in seeking to do this and to be as God desires us to be.

Why do some of us we think unforgiveness is okay? It probably harms us more than the person we choose not to forgive. When we harbor unforgiveness in our heart, it is displeasing to God. Our sin grieves the heart of God and the Holy Spirit, who lives within us. Not only is our fellowship with the person involved broken, but it is broken between God and us until we confess and repent. How very sad we would allow this to continue. We should do all that is possible to offer forgiveness and pray for reconciliation.

I realize there may be rare occasions where reconciliation may not be possible, even though one may try. The Bible says in Romans 12:18, "If it be possible, as much as lieth in you, live peaceably with all men." This verse recognizes that some may not accept your forgiveness or offer their own. But we are responsible for our actions before God, not another person's. Through the power of the Holy Spirit, you can still have peace, love, and forgiveness in your own heart.

Chapter 14
Joy

Have you ever seen a Christian who is so defeated when something goes wrong in their life? This should not happen to us since we have the power of God living within us. Pain, death of a loved one, difficult situations, illness, or anything else (and these will surely come) should not overwhelm us. We can be overcomers even during these times. How? Romans 8:37 tells us: "Nay, in all these things (referring to tribulation, distress, persecution, famine, nakedness, peril, or sword) we are more than conquerors through him that loved us." We can be light during these trying times through the power of the Holy Spirit. He can enable us to smile through the tears and to reflect Him.

1 John 5:4-5 reads, "For whosoever is born of God overcometh the world, and this is the victory that overcometh the world, even our faith. Who is he that overcometh the world, but he that believeth that Jesus is the Son of God?" Being born of God through our faith in Jesus Christ means we have all we need to overcome in difficult situations. We have the Holy Spirit to enable us and strengthen us. He will see us through any and all circumstances.

Philippians 4:19 says, "But my God shall supply all your need according to his riches in glory by Christ Jesus." As we look to Him in faith, we can be assured all our needs are covered. It does not say a bare minimum of supply, but according to His riches in glory. What a promise!

James 1:2-3 says, "My brethren, count it all joy when ye fall into various trials, knowing this, that the trial of your faith worketh patience." During great trial and pain, we are to count it joy. It does not say we will *feel* joy, but we are to count it as joy. We do that because God is working good out of it. The Bible tells us that we can always find something for which we can rejoice, something for which we are thankful. We can always look to Him in joy and thanksgiving that He knows what is happening; that He cares; that His strength is made perfect in our weakness, and that He will see us through. Isaiah 41:10 assures us, "Fear thou not; for I am with thee."

Don't waste today by letting life's pain or frustrations rob you of joy. Determine to be joyful anyway. Several years ago, I wrote this little poem:

> *"Capture a smile; put it on your face.*
> *Spread it around all over the place.*
> *Carry it with you wherever you go;*
> *and you'll never have a face that looks like sour dough."*

We can smile because we have the joy of the Lord within us. We have the joy of knowing Him. We have the joy of being His. Our faith, our joy in Him strengthens us.

Psalms 5:11 states, "But let all those who put their trust in thee rejoice; let them ever shout for joy because thou defendest them; let them also who love your name be joyful in thee." Even in the most trying of times, we can rejoice. God is with us. God is for us. This verse also says He defends us. What more could we ask?

Nehemiah 8:10d tells us that "the joy of the Lord is your strength." Isaiah 41:10: "Fear thou not; for I am with thee. Be not dismayed; for I am thy God. I will strengthen thee, yea, I will help thee; I will uphold thee with the right hand of my righteousness." We are not to fear or be dismayed by whatever the situation is. We are to fix our eyes on Him who loved us and gave himself for us. He will be our strength — our help — and He will hold us up.

Hebrews 12:2 says, "Looking unto Jesus, the author and finisher of our faith, who for the joy that was set before him endured the cross, despising the shame, and is set down at the right hand of the throne of God." Why did Jesus endure the cross and the shame? He did it 'for the joy that was set before him.' The joy set before Him must have been knowing He would be reunited in heaven with the Father and that He had obeyed and accomplished what God sent Him to do. We need to remember this when we are in a trial or experiencing a difficult situation. If we are faithful and obedient in these things, we can have the joy of knowing we have obeyed God and our actions are pleasing to Him.

God understands our grief when we lose a loved one. He watched His own son die on a cross. He knows; He understands. Death, illness, and painful trials come, but He is with us in them. Having joy does not mean we will never cry. Jesus wept at Lazarus' grave. We may cry when a loved one is dying or has died. But we won't cry like a person with no hope. The loss of someone we love is very sad, but hope is still there because we believe the truth of God's Word. Death is the door we pass through, but that door opens to life with Him forever. We can smile, even through the tears. We can be joyful that God is still on the throne. It is still "the day the Lord has made. Let us rejoice and be glad in it".

Chapter 15
Do Not Fear

"What time I am afraid, I will trust in thee" **(Psalm 56:3).**

This is the solution to fear — faith in the one who made us, who redeemed us, and claims us as His own. Do you remember when Peter walked on water? What happened when he took his eyes off of Jesus and looked at the stormy sea? He became afraid. And then remember what he did. He immediately looked back at Jesus in faith, asking Him to save him. This is what this verse is telling us. When we are afraid, look to Jesus. Trust in Him. Remember, we are never alone. God is always with us. He knows what is happening at any moment. May we look to Him in faith when fear and doubt come to us.

> *"Are not five sparrows sold for two farthings, and not one of them is forgotten before God? But even the hairs of your head are all numbered. Fear not, therefore; ye are of more value than many sparrows"* (Luke 12:6-7).

If God has so much care for sparrows, we should never fear. We are of more value than the sparrows, so much so that the hairs of our head are numbered. Wow! We really matter to God. Therefore, He will also take care of us.

Psalm 118:6a says, "The Lord is on my side; I will not fear." When the temptation to be afraid arises, recall God's Words. He is on our side. What more could we desire? We have the

God of heaven and earth, and all that is therein on our side. He tells us so himself!

Isaiah 51:7b states, "Fear not the reproach of men, neither be afraid of their revilings." Ah, we, as children of God, are certainly experiencing this reviling today, are we not? But, when God is with us and tells us we need not fear, the solution is simply to trust in Him. He is still in control. He is still on the throne. When Jesus was crucified, it seemed as though Satan and sin had won. But, no, this was all part of God's plan for our redemption. Christ rose from the grave triumphant and lives evermore to intercede for those of us who are His children. Could we be any more blessed!

Isaiah 43:1 tells us, "But, now, thus saith the Lord who created thee, O Jacob, and He who formed you, O Israel, Fear not; for I have redeemed thee, I have called thee by thy name; thou art mine." Also, Galatians 3:28 tells us there is neither Jew nor Greek, and we are all one in Christ Jesus. So, this verse speaks to all of God's people. He created us. He formed us. He redeemed us. And isn't it sweet and so special to know He calls us by our name? He tells us we are His! How special is that? Thank you, Jesus!

Isaiah 35:4 says, "Say to those of a fearful heart, Be strong, fear not; behold, your God will come with vengeance, even God, with a recompense; He will come and save you." Again, He tells not to fear. We need not worry nor fear because our glorious and wonderful God will come and save us. We should share this with others who have fearful hearts — those who are tempted to fear, as all of us are at times. We have His promise to rescue us. Look to Him.

Psalm 27:1 reminds us that "The Lord is my light and my salvation; whom shall I fear? The Lord is the strength of my life; of whom shall I be afraid?" This really makes one think. Is there anyone or anything we should fear knowing that God is our light, our salvation, and our strength? God himself is the strength of our life. He is sufficient for our every need.

Chapter 16
GOD IS SOVEREIGN

Whatever happens and whatever comes, God is sovereign. He is in control. There is never a time when He is not in control. When Jesus hung on the cross, it might have seemed that God was not in control. But He ordained that very act, that we might have forgiveness for our sins and be brought into a relationship with Him if we put our faith in Jesus Christ. He was still very much in control.

The book of Daniel states four times that God is in control:

> "..to the intent that the living may know that the Most High ruleth in the kingdom of men, and giveth it to whomsoever He will, and setteth up over it the basest of men" (Daniel 4:17b).

> "... till thou knowest that the Most High ruleth in the kingdom of men and giveth it to whomsoever He will" (Daniel 4:25d).

> "...until thou know that the Most High ruleth in the kingdom of men, and giveth it to whomsoever He will" (Daniel 4:32d).

> "And all the inhabitants of the earth are reputed as nothing; and He doeth according to his will in the army of heaven, and among the inhabitants of the earth, and none can stay his hand, or say unto him, what doest thou?" (Daniel 4:35).

These verses make it very clear that God is in control at all times and everywhere.

Yes, He does allow us free will sometimes and in some things. For instance, even as His children, He does not make us obey Him. He gives us free will to obey or disobey. However, it is to our shame and pain if we choose to disobey. At some point, His chastisement will surely come. But, note that little word *allow*. He allows it. Just because He allows something does not mean He is not in control. The very fact that He allowed it shows His sovereignty.

Daniel 2:21 reads, "And He changeth the times and the seasons; He removeth kings, and setteth up kings." God is in control of the times and the seasons. He is in control of kings. He wills or allows who sits on the throne.

Romans 13:1b makes it clear that "for there is no power but of God; the powers that be are ordained of God." We should never underestimate the power of God nor His control of what is happening. Sometimes He gives us the leadership we deserve. Often, He gives us the good that we don't deserve.

Psalms 103:19 says, "The Lord hath prepared his throne in the heavens; and his kingdom ruleth over all." God is in control. This should give us great comfort. God knows. He cares. He will work it out. He is with us and for us.

> *"God, who made the world and all things in it, seeing that He is Lord of heaven and earth, dwelleth not in temples made with hands, neither is worshiped with men's hands, as though He needed anything, seeing He giveth to all life, and breath, and all things; and hath made of one blood all nations of men to dwell on all the face of the earth; and hath determined the times before appointed, and the bounds of their habitation"* **(Acts 17:24).**

God is in control of our times and the bounds of our life and even where we live. Nothing can come to us that God does not either will or allow. During difficulties or pain, it is comforting to know that God knows all about it and to know that there is a reason, or, I believe, a purpose in it. Again, it is comforting to know that God is in control. We know He is somehow working good out of it.

Chapter 16
STAND STRONG AND PRAY

In the Old Testament, the nation of Israel would sometimes stray from the Lord. When that happened, God's judgment would come to them. As a nation, America is straying from God is so many ways. As judgment came to Israel, it will also surely come to America unless we repent.

We need to pray that God would grant us a spiritual awakening in the hearts of us, His people, and in this nation. We should pray that individuals would come to know Jesus as their Savior and Lord. Pray that America would again become a nation 'whose God is the Lord.'

Pray for open hearts in our leaders in this country and in the rest of the world, that they may put their faith in Jesus Christ. Pray that God would grant them wisdom in their hearts and minds to make good and wise decisions.

> *"I exhort, therefore, that first of all, supplications, prayers, intercessions, and giving of thanks, be made for all men, for kings, and for all that are in authority, that we may lead a quiet and peaceable life in all godliness and honesty"* **(In 1 Timothy 2:1-2).**

We are told to pray for all men and for all that are in authority. I don't really see where this is an option. Yet, today, instead of seeing or hearing a lot of this, we see excessive hate spewing forth, especially from some of the leadership in our country. We also see this same hatred from some who carry the name

"Christian." We wonder how that can be. This scripture does not say to pray for those in authority only if we like them. It simply says, "pray for them."

I might add that it goes beyond praying for the leaders in our own country. It says to pray for kings and all that are in authority. That means we should pray for leaders over all the world. These verses also tell us why we are to pray for them. It is for our own good. We pray and desire that we may lead a quiet and peaceful life in godliness and honesty. Do we not desire that? Do we not want good and wise leadership for our country? Or are we more concerned about aligning with our political party? If this is the case, and I do believe it is at times, then we really should be on our knees before God. We need to pray not only for our country's leaders but also for ourselves, that God would help us to humble ourselves before Him and obey Him and His Word in praying for those in authority.

Yes, there have been presidents that I did not like nor vote for. This was, among other things, because of their stand for things against God's Word. But, once they were elected, I did pray for them. Did I 'feel' like praying for them? No, but as stated before, we make choices in our walk with God to either obey or disobey. So, it was a choice I made in obedience to Him. Even if you think of it in non-spiritual terms, it is the sensible thing to do. It is our country, and whatever happens affects us.

Before the election, we have every right as citizens of America to campaign for or against whomever we choose. Although, as children of God, we should never walk in that voting booth having made these decisions all on our own. As in all things, we should have already sought the will of God in making an important decision. We should also consider the answer to this question: are they for us as God's people or against us? I don't mean *for us* to the point of discrimination. What I actually mean is will they protect our right of freedom to worship and obey God as is afforded us in the Constitution? If they are not one to do this, you can be sure they are not believers in Jesus Christ.

That means their authority and decisions will not uphold God or His Word. Instead, they will be against it. They may carry the name Christian, but if they stand against His Word, they are certainly not walking in obedience to Him

Just because they seek to protect freedom of religion does not necessarily mean they are Christians. But it does mean they will not rule or fight against the things of God. They will not seek to take away religious freedom. Let us pray for ourselves, that we, as God's redeemed children, may seek and know His wisdom before we walk into that voting booth. I can assure you that Satan is pleased when we walk into that booth and vote our way without seeking God's will. He loves it when we vote for those who support his agenda.

Once the election is over, we have the responsibility before God to pray for whoever is elected, whether it is our candidate or otherwise. Why would we not pray for them? As mentioned before, I admit sometimes it is difficult to pray for a particular person in office. Why is it difficult? Because we are letting our emotions rule. We should not make our decisions based on emotions. Our decision should always be to obey God. We decide to obey God and to pray for that person because God tells us to do so. It also makes sense. Why would we not want them to succeed? Why would we not pray for them to do well? The job they do, good or bad, will eventually affect us in probably more ways than we think. Therefore, common sense tells us to pray for them. Even more important is the fact that God has commanded us to do so, as shown in 1 Timothy 2.

The world does not seem to understand that someday all of us will stand before God. They seem to think they are like the Titanic, a ship that was believed to be invincible. They do not realize how quickly everything we have—even our very life—can be taken away. When I think of 9-11, I am reminded of how quickly man's accomplishment can be brought to nothing, of how, without God, we are nothing. All that we do is nothing unless He is the heart of it.

We need to stand strong for the Word of God, even when we are accused of being judgmental and not loving. Those accusations are a ploy to throw the focus back on us and away from those opposed to the truth of the Bible. God's Word is truth, and to stand firmly on it does have a lot to do with love. It has to do with our love for God and the truth of the Bible. We are not judgmental when we agree with that which God has already declared to be sin. We simply agree with Him. To affirm wrong actions is not love. Love speaks the truth. Love does not condone sin. Love confronts. We are not doing anyone a favor by allowing someone to think something is okay when the Bible tells us it isn't. When we do not confront, we are disobedient to God, because we are called to be salt and light. We are not called to help hide or cover up sin. We are called to be light. And light never covers; light exposes.

Sadly, we see some Christians today who waver on this in the name of love. I do not see anywhere in the Bible where we can straddle the fence. There are only two sides, God's or Satan's. Jesus says in Matthew 12:30a that "He that is not with me is against me." We can either stand strongly for and on God's Word, or we stand with Satan. It's our choice.

We should not hold too tightly our possessions or even our loved ones. Everything we have is from God and belongs to Him. We need to hold on to Him and not our possessions or even our loved ones. Love our loved ones, yes, but God comes before those we love. Everyone is His to take whenever it pleases Him, and we should commit all of them to Him. Sometimes we may have to do like Abraham did and place them on a figurative altar, giving them to God, knowing we can trust Him with their lives as we continue to pray. We need to labor for Him and not for things. Yes, we have to work to live, but money and possessions should not become our god.

We need to be in His Word. The Holy Spirit takes the Word in us and uses it. He will use it to strengthen us and our faith in Him to help us stand in difficult and trying times. It teaches us how God wants us to live and the type of person He wants us to be. We don't know what we will face in days to come, or what our children and grandchildren will have to face. All of us need to be grounded in God's Word.

Whatever comes to us, one thing is sure. 1 John 4-4 says, "Greater is He that is in you, than he that is in the world." We are God's children, and He has promised in Hebrews 13:5 that "I will never leave you nor forsake you." In addition, Psalms 37:18-19 reads, "The Lord knows the days of the upright and their inheritance shall be forever. They shall not be ashamed in the evil times, and in the days of famine, they shall be satisfied." This verse reminds me of God's faithfulness shown in 1 Kings 17:6 when God had the ravens to feed Elijah when there was no food. God will provide for our every need.

> *"But the salvation of the righteous is of the Lord; He is their strength in the time of trouble. And the Lord shall help them and deliver them. He shall deliver them from the wicked and save them because they trust in him"* **(Psalms 37:39).**

This is a reminder that we are never left on our own. We are not alone when trouble comes. The scripture tells us that God is our strength. He will help us and deliver us. That is His promise, and His promises are sure and true. Psalms 37:10-11 says, "For yet a little while and the wicked shall not be; yea thou shalt diligently consider his place and it shall not be. But the meek shall inherit the earth and shall delight themselves in the abundance of peace." Hold that thought. The day is coming when we shall delight ourselves in the abundance of peace in His presence forever.

These are great and precious promises from God. His Word is full of promises for you and me and for those of us who are His through faith in Jesus Christ.

May we pray for our church, the body of Christ. Let us pray for one another "that ye (we) may be blameless and harmless;

children of God, without rebuke in the midst of a crooked and perverse nation, among whom ye shine as lights in the world, holding forth the Word of life" (Philippians 2:13-16a).

Chapter 17
Unlovely People

Do you know unlovely people? Most of us know some. If you don't, I can introduce you to a few! In my lifetime, I feel I've had my share. When I came to a certain place in my walk with the Lord, I realized I had probably asked for it. When I was around thirty-six years old, I began praying for God to give me the gift of agape love. As He began to work this in me, I looked back over all those unlovely people who had come into my life (some were still there), and I realized that God had always known I would someday pray for the gift of love. He actually started working ahead of time by bringing those unlovely ones into my life. He was beginning to teach me even before I knew or asked. I suppose He also knew I would be a slow learner! But what a glorious God He is, who anticipated my need before I even recognized it within myself.

Before I go further, I need to make it clear that He is still working on me. I certainly have not arrived, but I am so thankful that God doesn't give up on me.

I do not think I have ever prayed for someone I had a problem with that God didn't also point back to me and my attitude. He reminds me that I also need to pray for myself. This reproving is one of the ministries of the Holy Spirit. I am so thankful He does that, and I am not left on my own.

Years ago, a 'friend' hopped on my case because I failed to do something exactly when or how they wanted it. I allowed them to 'let me have it' and said nothing. But I can assure you that what I was feeling was anything but 'nothing.' Later, on my way home, I seethed with anger. I told God they had no right and how wrong they were in what was said. This was the answer I received: "You should be praying for them. They are the one who has the problem. It's only your problem if you allow it to become one." Isn't that what we do so often? We allow someone else to upset us and destroy our peace due to their insecurities or whatever the cause may be. God's message to me that day delivered me from allowing someone to disturb and disrupt me and my peace. Once I prayed for cleansing and forgiving of my attitude, I could then pray for them and their attitude. Although, I must confess I am still not perfect in this. I am sorry to say I still struggle with this sometimes, but God is always here to remind me. Thank you, Lord.

Another example is when I was praying for someone and their hateful disposition. In doing this, I stated to God, "I am so glad that I'm not like her." Immediately, God brought to mind the scripture in Luke 18:9-13. This is a parable about the Pharisee and the tax collector who were praying. The Pharisee thanked God that he was not like other people. He told God all about his goodness and all the things he did. The tax collector, in much humility, prayed for God's mercy. The Holy Spirit made me see myself as that Pharisee. Humbling? You had better believe it! Again, this called for my repentance. I did continue to pray for her, but not with my 'holier than thou' attitude.

That doesn't mean God thought it was acceptable to be like this person. What it does mean is that I was not to consider myself superior in any way. If we, as God's children, are hopefully different, it is because of nothing we have done. It is the work of the Holy Spirit within us. 1 Corinthians 4:7 states:

> *"For who maketh thee to differ from another? And what hast thou that thou didst not receive? Now, if thou didst receive it, why dost thou glory, as if thou didst not receive it?"*

This verse is telling us that God is the one who makes us different. It is not something we did. It is something we received. All the honor and glory go to God along with our thanksgiving.

Now when I pray for someone who always seems to bring out the 'beast' in me, God reminds me of my responsibility to agape love them and points out my own shortcomings. Therefore, I end up praying for myself as much as for them.

Chapter 18
How Should We Live?

"If ye then, be risen with Christ, seek those things which are above, where Christ sitteth on the right hand of God. Set your affections on things above, not on things on the earth" (Colossians 3:1-2).

Think of life as being on a faraway car trip. On the way, you may stop and see many beautiful things and beautiful scenery. You may also have a flat tire, a car breakdown of some kind, possibly even an accident. But in all this, the good and the bad, always in the front of your mind is your destination. You are anticipating your arrival. I think that is what God is telling us here. We have much to do here, but always in the front of our minds should be our destination. We are to keep our eyes on Him, our hearts and minds thinking on Him and His Word, looking forward to being with Him and the joy that is set before us.

Further in Colossians 3:3-4, it reads, "For ye are dead, and your life is hidden with Christ in God. When Christ, who is our life, shall appear, then shall ye also appear with him in glory." This, along with "If ye, then, be risen with Christ," in verse 1, is our position. Positionally, we have died to sin; our life is hidden with Christ in God, and we shall appear with Him in glory. Our position is plainly declared—risen with Christ, and our life is hidden with Him in God. That does not change. It is assurance we are His.

Colossians 3: 5-9 says, "Mortify, therefore, your members which are upon the earth: fornication, uncleanness, inordinate affection, evil desire, and covetousness (which is idolatry) for which things' sake the wrath of God cometh upon the sons of disobedience; in the which ye also once walked, when ye lived in them. But now ye also put off all these: anger, wrath, malice, blasphemy, filthy communication out of your mouth. Lie not to one another, seeing that ye have put off the old man with his deeds."

This refers to our walk. Notice that it says "your members which are upon the earth"; not hidden with Christ in God; not risen with Him as mentioned in verses three and four. We are to live as though dead to sin. We are to mortify evil desires that work in our flesh. Those evil desires are equated with idolatry — deifying self and what we want more than or instead of God.

Colossians 3:10 says, "And have put on the new man, that is renewed in knowledge after the image of him that created him, where there is neither Greek nor Jew, circumcision nor uncircumcision, barbarian, Scythian, bond nor free, but Christ is all and in all." As we put off these sins and put on the new man, we are being renewed in knowledge and molded in His image. He tells us that in this new creation, all distinctions, including race, position, or status, vanish. We are all on the same level. Christ is everything and everywhere to all believers with no respect of persons.

Colossians 3:12-14 reads, "Put on, therefore, as the elect of God, holy and beloved, tender mercies, kindness, humbleness of mind, meekness, long-suffering; forbearing one another, and forgiving one another, if any man have a quarrel against any; even as Christ forgave you, so also do ye. And above all these things, put on love, which is the bond of perfectness." I repeat, this is only possible when we are fully surrendered to God and the Holy Spirit within us. Then, through His help and His power, we can do and be these things. He gives us the power to love, to forgive, and to endure whatever comes with good temper. We can agape love someone not because of whom they are or their actions. We can love them as Christ loved us. He loved us while we were still sinners.

Second Corinthians 5:20 speaks of us being ambassadors for Christ. Let us think about that. When the United States sends an ambassador to a foreign country, this ambassador represents our nation and our leaders. They represent our country—what we stand for and what we believe. The foreign nation's perception of that ambassador is how they will think of us as a nation. The same is true of us as Christians. How do people see us as we live out our lives? Are we good ambassadors for Christ? Are we giving the world a true picture of what He is like, or are we giving a false picture? How much love do we have or do we give? The Bible says that the world will know believers by the love we have for one another. Does the world see love in you and in me?

As ambassadors for Christ, we need to live the resurrected life. How do we do that? Keeping rules or obeying the law will never change the person. It will not give us new life. We cannot live a new or resurrected life on our own, regardless of how hard we try. Living the resurrected life happens only through the power of the Holy Spirit. Christ not only redeemed us from the penalty of sin, but He gives us the power to be different than we were before He came to live within us. He will live in and through us if we allow Him to do so.

He does not make us obey Him. What will make a person want to obey and to please someone? One word: love. If we truly love someone, we want to please them. This is stated plainly in John 14-21: "He that hath my commandments, and keepeth them, he it is that loveth me; and he that loveth me shall be loved of my Father, and I will love him, and will manifest (make known) myself to him." The more we love Him, the more we obey. The more we obey, the greater awareness we have of Him in our hearts and lives.

Verse 15 of Colossians 3 tells us, "And let the peace of God rule in your hearts, to which also ye are called in one body, and be ye thankful." I will emphasize the word *let*—meaning to allow. Have you ever thought of some of these things as a choice? His peace rules in us as we allow Him control of our hearts, our wills, and our lives. We should not allow another person or situation to agitate us and rob us of our peace. We cannot allow unforgiveness or lack of love to steal our peace. Forgive freely and love freely.

We are also told to be thankful. Instead of allowing our minds to dwell on things that irritate or worry us, let us think on the many things for which we can be thankful, giving God thanks for all He has given us in Christ Jesus.

Colossians 3:16 says, "Let the word of Christ dwell in you richly, in all wisdom teaching and admonishing one another, in Psalms and hymns and spiritual songs singing with grace in your hearts to the Lord." For the Word to dwell in us, we have to read, study, and meditate on it often. Make a habit of letting His Word dwell in our hearts and minds, of singing to and of the Lord, always with thanksgiving to Him.

Colossians 3:17 states, "And whatever ye do in word or deed, do all in the name of the Lord Jesus, giving thanks to God and the Father by him." Following His will and the word of God, everything we do, we are to do in His name. We will find in life that some things are done much easier if we do them as unto Him. In doing so, we can do them more joyfully. As we do them in His name, we are also told to give thanks to Him. We can thank Him and give Him all the glory, honor and praise.

Galatians 6:8-9 says, "And let us not be weary in well doing; for in due season we shall reap, if we faint not. As we have therefore, opportunity, let us do good to all men, especially unto to them who are of the household of faith." God is exhorting us not to grow weary in serving others. He also makes us aware that we are to serve all people as we are given the opportunity.

As believers, we are ambassadors for Christ. That is our mission. May we be the best ambassadors possible—yielding ourselves to him, and presenting our bodies "a living sacrifice, holy, acceptable unto God, which is your (our) reasonable service."

Titus 2:11-14 says, "For the grace of God that bringeth salvation hath appeared to all men, teaching us that denying ungodliness and worldly lust, we should live soberly, righteously, and godly in this present age, looking for that blessed hope, and the glorious appearing of the great God and our Savior, Jesus Christ, who gave himself for us that He might redeem us from all iniquity, and purify unto himself a people of his own, zealous of good works." God wants us to live according to His Word and to walk in fellowship with Him as we look for His return. He wants us to be looking for 'the glorious appearing of our great God and Savior, Jesus Christ.'

Luke 21:27-28 reads, "And then shall they see the Son of man coming in a cloud, with power and great glory. And when these things begin to come to pass, then look up, and lift up your heads for your redemption draweth near." Every day we live is a little closer to that day. He may or may not come in our lifetime. If not, our redemption will come on whatever day He calls us home.

Hebrews 9:28b says, "…and unto them that look for him shall He appear the second time without sin unto salvation." He wants us to look for His return. Do we live in anticipation of His return? Do we look for Him? He will come in power and great glory. His return will be glorious, indeed. Even so, come, Lord Jesus!

Chapter 19
HOPE

What is hope? The dictionary describes it as a feeling that what is wanted will happen; a desire accompanied by expectation. Romans 8:24 states, "For we are saved by hope. But hope that is seen is not hope. For what a man seeth, why doth he yet hope for?" Hope is not something we already see or know. It is something we look for, something God has promised us. We are certain of this hope because He is trustworthy. Numbers 23:19 assures us that "God is not a man that He should lie; neither the son of man that He should repent. Hath He said and shall He not do it? Or hath He spoken, and shall He not make it good?" That which God has promised, He will do.

Hebrews 6:18-19b: "That by two immutable things, in which it was impossible for God to lie, we might have a strong consolation, who have fled for refuge to lay hold upon the hope set before us: which hope we have as an anchor of the soul, both sure and steadfast." We are again assured that God cannot and does not lie. Our soul is anchored by and in this hope. We are also assured that the hope we have in Him is sure and steadfast. These verses tell us these things are immutable. That means they are never changing or varying; unchangeable. God said it and His Word is truth. You can count on it.

1 Thessalonians 5:8-9 speaks of putting on "the breastplate of faith and love, and for an helmet, the hope of salvation. For God hath not appointed us to wrath, but to obtain salvation by our Lord Jesus Christ." I believe the helmet is the provision of

and protection for the hope of our salvation we have in Him.

Romans 12:11-12 says we are to "be fervent in spirit; serving the Lord; rejoicing in hope." As we serve the Lord, being fervent in spirit, we can rejoice in the sure hope that is set before us.

Romans 5:1-2 "Therefore, being justified by faith, we have peace with God through our Lord Jesus Christ, by whom also we have access by faith into this grace in which we stand, and rejoice in hope of the glory of God." Verse 5: "And hope maketh not ashamed, because the love of God is shed abroad in our hearts by the Holy Spirit, who is given unto us." We will never be ashamed of our hope in the Lord. He is with us and in us. Therefore, we can rejoice in the sure hope we have in Him.

Romans 15:13 reads, "Now the God of hope fill you with all joy and peace in believing, that ye may abound in hope, through the power of the Holy Spirit." It is wonderful to know that we can abound in hope and have joy and peace through our God and the power of the Holy Spirit. There is nothing too hard for Him.

Psalms 147:11: "The Lord takes pleasure in those who fear him; those who hope in his mercy." What a beautiful and humbling thing to know that God takes pleasure in us because we place our hope in Him and in His mercy.

1 Peter 1:3-4: "Blessed be God and Father of our Lord Jesus Christ, who, according to his abundant mercy, hath begotten us again unto a living hope by the resurrection of Jesus Christ from the dead, to an inheritance incorruptible, and undefiled, and that fadeth not away, reserved in heaven for you, who are kept by the power of God through faith unto salvation."

Wow! Those two verses pack a lot—God's abundant mercy; a hope that is alive and living; an incorruptible, undefiled inheritance reserved in heaven for us. This is all available to us and to those who believe in the Lord Jesus Christ. It also says we are kept by the power of God through faith unto salvation. What a blessing to hear that we are kept by God himself. That makes it a very, very sure thing! Can we ever praise Him enough for who He is and for all He has given us in Christ Jesus? Probably not, but we can try!

Psalms 119:49-50 reads, "Remember the Word unto thy servant, upon which thou hast caused me to hope. This is my comfort in my affliction; for thy Word hath given me life." Here the Psalmist urges God to remember His Word and His promises, upon which he hopes. We also place our hopes in God and His Word. It will be comforting for us in any and all situations. It strengthens us, sustains us, and uplifts us.

1 John 3:2-3: "Beloved, now are we the children of God, and it doth not yet appear what we shall be, but we know that when we see him, we shall be like him, for we shall see him as he is. And every man that hath this hope in him purifieth himself even as he is pure." Have you ever thought that our hope in Him is purifying us? He is working in us in ways of which we are not even aware. God's Word is so rich and so laden with treasures. But to find and know them, we have to be in the Word, looking for and learning them. These verses also tell us that someday we will be like Him. This is possible through the love of God and the sacrifice of Jesus Christ.

Jeremiah 17:7: "Blessed is the man who trusteth in the Lord, and whose hope the Lord is." We are blessed when we place our faith and our hope in the Lord. We are most blessed by Him of all people and in so many ways.

Psalms 119: 49-50: "Remember the word unto thy servant, upon which thou hast caused me to hope. This is my comfort in my affliction, for thy word hath given me life." We can remind God of His promises and His word that He has given us. Our hope and His word are a comfort to us in difficult situations. God has provided for our every need.

Galatians 5:5: "For we through the Spirit wait for the hope of righteousness by faith." Now we wait in hope, but someday we will be with Him in eternity as that hope becomes a reality and "so shall we ever be with the Lord." All praise, honor, and glory be to the Father, the Son, and the Holy Spirit.

Chapter 20
THANKSGIVING AND PRAISE

How often do we thank God for something, for anything? And how often do we praise Him? Do we neglect this most important part of our spiritual life? If so, God grant that from this day forward, this will change.

> *"And as He (Jesus) entered into a certain village, there met him ten men that were lepers, who stood afar off. And they lifted up their voice, and said, Jesus, Master, have mercy on us. And when He saw them, He said unto them, Go shew yourselves unto the priest. And it came to pass that, as they went, they were cleansed. And one of them, when he saw that he was healed, turned back and with a loud voice glorified God. And fell down at his feet, giving him thanks, and he was a Samaritan. And, Jesus answering, said, Were there not ten cleansed? But where are the nine? They are not found that returned to give glory to God, except this stranger"* (Luke 17:12-18).

Ten were cleansed and healed, but only one glorified God and returned to give Him thanks. Do we do that sometimes? Do we fail to give thanks when it is due? Do we fail to give glory to God? God grant that we do not fail in this way. Should we fail, let us today resolve to become more acutely aware always to thank and praise God, asking the Holy Spirit to help us do this.

Let's see some passages from God's Word on thanksgiving

and praise. And shall we start with the more difficult scriptures? I don't mean to imply the scripture itself is difficult. *We* are difficult, as it is often hard to get self out of the way, even in praying.

Ephesians 5:20 says, "Giving thanks always for all things unto God and the Father, in the name of our Lord Jesus Christ." 1 Thessalonians 5:18 reads, "In everything give thanks, for this is the will of God in Christ Jesus concerning you." How easy is that? Not at all. It doesn't seem to be, right? How do we give thanks in difficult and trying situations? How do we give thanks in the middle of pain and illness? How can we feel thankful when we see a loved one dying from lung cancer and struggling to breathe or in terrible pain? How can we be thankful when our heart is breaking as we see a loved one walking in disobedience to God and living a life of sin?

Remember we pointed out earlier that so much of our Christian life is a choice? This is another example. We may not feel thankful in some situations. Indeed, we almost surely will not. But we can give thanks by an act of our will. We choose to give God thanks in obedience to His Word. We know that God is sovereign. That tells us that God either wills or allows difficult situations to come. So, by either willing or allowing it, that means He is working, or will work good out of it as He promises in Romans 8:28. This is why we can thank Him, because we know His Word is true, and we know He is faithful to work good out of it.

Colossians 3:17: "And whatever ye do in word or deed, do all in the name of the Lord Jesus, giving thanks to God and the Father by him." All that we do in word or deed, according to God's will, we are to do in God's name and through the power of His Holy Spirit. Whatever we do, we are to be thankful we can do it through the health, the strength, and the means that He has given us; through the knowledge He gives, and through the opportunities He brings to us. Let us always acknowledge that we are just the vessels through whom God works as we obey Him. It is He who gives us these opportunities to serve. It is another thing for which we can be thankful.

Hebrews 13:15 says, "By him, therefore, let us offer the sacrifice of praise to God continually, that is, the fruit of our lips giving thanks to his name." In addition, Psalms 116:17: "I will offer to thee the sacrifice of thanksgiving, and will call upon the name of the Lord."

Have you ever thought of praise or giving thanks as being a sacrifice? What exactly does that mean? Could it mean when we are confronted with something we don't like, we 'sacrifice' how we feel and give praise and thanks to God, anyway? We mentioned earlier about thanking God when our hearts are breaking for a loved one who is walking in disobedience to Him. Is this not a sacrifice of thanksgiving and praise as we yield them and their situation to God, who loves them even more than we do? Are we willing to put aside our feelings to be obedient to Him, knowing He has a plan and a purpose in allowing this? Can we give Him thanks and praise because we trust Him to work good out of it? Can we not trust our loving God to bring them back to Him? Ephesians 3:20 tells us that He "is able to do exceedingly abundantly above all that we ask or think, according to the power that worketh in us." Hear and absorb what this verse says. He is more than able! I guarantee you when we ignore how we feel and give Him thanks and give Him praise in spite of these feelings and do this in sincerity, we will *feel* much better.

Psalms 107:8: "Oh, that we would praise the Lord for his goodness, and for his wonderful works in the children of men." Do we remember to praise Him just because He is good? Can we praise Him because He is Lord of heaven and Lord of the earth? Can we praise Him because He is holy, just, faithful, and that He loves us and calls us His children? Are we not thankful for that among His many other attributes? Do we thank and praise Him for the wonderful work He does in our children, in our neighbors' children, in our friends' children, and yes, in us?

Psalms 95:2: "Let us come before his presence with thanksgiving." How often do we do this? Or how often do we come to Him with only our cares and our needs? How often do we thank Him for loving us? How often do we thank Him for Jesus, through whom we have forgiveness of sin and, without whom, we would be lost and headed for hell? How often do we thank Him for the Holy Spirit who lives within us, who is the comforter, the Spirit of truth, the one the Bible says will teach us all things, and the one who will guide us into all truth? Should we not begin every prayer in thanksgiving for these things?

Psalms 100:4: "Enter into his gates with thanksgiving, and into his courts with praise; let us be thankful unto him, and bless his name." If we do not already do this, may we resolve today to begin. Ask the Holy Spirit to bring to remembrance our resolution that we may always come into His presence with thanksgiving and praise to Him. We can praise Him for other things, yes, but may we remember to give Him praise for who He is — almighty God. He is love. He is glorious, righteous, mighty, merciful, sovereign, all-wise. He is the great I AM, the creator, the maker of heaven and earth, and all that is therein. He is the Alpha and the Omega. And that doesn't even begin to describe Him. He is our Lord and our God, our fortress, our mighty tower, our refuge, our help in trouble, our light, our salvation, our rock, and so much more.

Every day, there is so much to thank Him for if we just remember to watch. We can thank Him for health, friends, family, home, food, His presence with us and in us, His love, His mercy, and His grace, His protection and safety, and so much more.

When we write a check to be placed in the church offering plate, do we remember to give Him thanks that we have the opportunity and the blessing to give? Do we remember that all we give is from the blessing of all that He has given to us? Do we remember "that every good and perfect gift is from above, and cometh down from the Father of lights, with whom is no variableness, neither shadow of turning"? (James 1:17).

Psalms 34:1 says, "I will bless the Lord at all times; his praise shall continually be in my mouth." Can you imagine how different we would be if this were true in each of us? Praise and worship are not only pleasing to God, but they also lift us up as we raise our voices and our hearts in praise and adoration to Him. Do we realize that we can praise Him anywhere and at any time? We do not have to be in church or any particular place. He is with us wherever we are. We can praise Him in the car, in the shower, as we mop the floor, as we walk down the street, as we gaze at the stars. Whether verbally or silently, we can lift our praise to Him from hearts full of love for Who He is and all He has given to us through Christ Jesus, our Lord and Savior.

Give Him all the praise and all the glory because He and He alone is worthy. Psalms 150:6 confirms, "Let everything that hath breath praise the Lord. Praise ye the Lord."

Chapter 21
Seasons of Life

I often think of our life being much like the four seasons we have here in North Carolina. Winters are cold, bleak, and with less sunshine than other seasons. Many of the trees have lost their leaves. They are barren and look much like they are dead. I compare that to our lives before we come to know Jesus Christ. Our lives are somewhat barren or bleak, and we are spiritually dead in our trespasses and sin.

Then spring comes. It is not as cold, and we have more sunshine. The days are warmer. Trees began to show buds of coming leaves. It seems new life is beginning. Isn't that what happens when we receive Jesus into our hearts and lives? We are 'budding.' We are beginning a new and different life in Him. We are beginning to grow as His children. We are growing in the knowledge of Him and His Word. Wait. There is more!

Summer has now arrived. The days are much, much warmer. The trees are no longer budding but are now full and green with new leaves. Each year they grow more until they reach full maturity. I think of this as our maturing or growing season in our walk with God. We are mature in that relationship with Him but will continue to grow and mature even more in the years ahead.

Fall is now here. The days are pleasant and begin to get somewhat cooler. Leaves on the trees begin to show bright and brilliant colors. They are absolutely beautiful. They have reached their peak in growth and beauty. Soon they will begin to fall from the trees, but this season will go out in a blaze of glorious color. Hopefully, that's what our life will be like when we are in our last days here on this earth. May we be at our peak and our very best in our walk and relationship with God. May our lives be so beautiful and shining for and through Him that He takes us out in a blaze of His glory! Shine, Jesus, shine!

Chapter 22
HOME

'Home' at the end of our life is one of two places. It is either heaven or hell. Whether we believe or do not believe, this is truth. For those of us who believe, heaven will be our home. For those who do not believe, who have rejected Jesus Christ, hell will be their home. This does not come from me. It comes from God Himself in His Word, the Holy Bible.

For those of us who believe, this is our coming home:

> *"I go to prepare a place for you. And if I go and prepare a place for you, I will come again, and receive you unto myself, that where I am, there ye may be also"* (John 14:2-3).

Jesus himself has prepared a place for us. He also made way for us to go there and be with Him. He says in verse 6, "I am the way, the truth, and the life; no man cometh unto the Father, but by me."

1 John 3:2: "Beloved, now are we the children of God, and it doth not yet appear what we shall be, but we know that, when He shall appear, we shall be like him; for we shall see him as he is." What a glorious thought that someday we shall be like Him.

> *"Arise, shine, for thy light is come, and the glory of the Lord is risen upon thee. For, behold, the darkness shall cover the earth, and gross darkness the peoples, but the Lord shall arise upon*

> thee, and his glory shall be seen upon thee...The sun shall no more be thy light by day, neither for brightness shall the moon give light unto thee; but the Lord shall be unto thee an everlasting light, and thy God and thy glory. The sun shall no more go down, neither shall the moon withdraw itself; for the Lord shall be thine everlasting light, and the days of thy mourning shall be ended" (Isaiah 60:1-2, 19-20).

We have so much to look forward to and so much for which to give thanks and praise.

1 Corinthians 2:9 says, "Eye hath not seen, nor ear heard, neither have entered into the heart of man, the things which God hath prepared for them that love him." We cannot imagine what it will be like to see Him face to face. We cannot imagine what He has prepared for us, but it will be glorious. There will be no sin there, just joyous peace and love with and for God the Father, God the Son, and God the Holy Spirit. What a blessed time it will be. God will be our all in all.

Romans 8:18 reads, "For I reckon that the sufferings of this present time are not worthy to be compared with the glory that shall be revealed in us." A better day is coming. Look for it. Wait for it. In God's way and in His time, it will come. Romans 11:36 states, "For of him and through him, and to him, are all things: to whom be glory forever. Amen."

> "And I heard a great voice out of heaven saying, Behold, the tabernacle of God is with men, and He will dwell with them, and they shall be his people, and God himself shall be with them, and be their God. And God shall wipe away all tears from their eyes; and there shall be no more death, neither sorrow, nor crying, neither shall there be any more pain, for the former things are passed away" (Revelation 21:3-4).

Someday we will never again experience pain. We will never

again experience death, tears, sorrow, or crying, for God himself will have wiped away all of our tears. We will have the joy of being with Him throughout eternity.

> *"And I saw no temple in it; for the Lord God Almighty and the Lamb are the temple of it. And the city had no need of the sun, neither of the moon, to shine it in; for the glory of the Lord did light it and the Lamb is the lamp of it. And the nations of them who are saved shall walk in the light of it, and the kings of the earth do bring their glory and honor into it. And the gates of it shall not be shut at all by day; for there shall be no night there"* **(Revelation 21:22-25).**

Ah, do we remember our destination? Do we look forward to the day when we will be with our Lord and Savior forevermore? Remind us, Lord, that we are traveling to a destination. We are traveling to be with you – all made possible through the death, burial, and resurrection of our Lord Jesus Christ! Praise the Lamb that was slain forevermore!

Revelation 22:3-4: "And there shall be no more curse, but the throne of God and the Lamb shall be in it, and his servants shall serve him; and they shall see his face, and his name shall be in their foreheads." Revelation 22:17: "And the Spirit and the bride say, Come. And let him that heareth say, Come. And let him that is athirst come. And whosoever will, let him take the water of life freely."

Revelation 22:20: "He that testifieth these things saith, Surely, I come quickly. Amen. Even so come, Lord Jesus."

There is still time. "Whosoever will, let him take of the water of life freely." The invitation is there for whosoever will come to Jesus in repentance and faith. Come; receive forgiveness of sin; come and look forward to new life now in and with Jesus Christ. Come and look forward to someday being 'home' forever. Come and go where there is no more sin, pain, nor sorrow; no more crying; and no more death. Come where there will be joy and peace with Him forevermore. Come, be with Him who "so loved the world [that includes you and me] that He gave his only begotten son, that whosoever believeth in him should not perish, but have everlasting life."

www.ingramcontent.com/pod-product-compliance
Lightning Source LLC
Chambersburg PA
CBHW021118080526
44587CB00010B/564